ART, VISION, and SYMMETRY

The HIDDEN GEOMETRY of FRANK LLOYD WRIGHT

John H. Shoaff

MISSION POINT PRESS
TRAVERSE CITY, MICHIGAN

Art, Vision, and Symmetry
The Hidden Geometry of Frank Lloyd Wright

By John H. Shoaff

Readers are encouraged to go to www.MissionPointPress.com to contact the author or to find information on how to buy this book in bulk at discounted rates.

Published by Mission Point Press, Traverse City, Michigan
2554 Chandler Road
Traverse City, MI 49696

First edition, first printing
ISBN: 978-1-943338-05-4

Library of Congress Control Number: 2019918396

Printed in the United States of America.

To Julie.

ART, VISION, and SYMMETRY:

The HIDDEN GEOMETRY of FRANK LLOYD WRIGHT

JOHN H. SHOAFF

CONTENTS

PREFACE

I arrived in Paris in just time for the Parcours des mondes, an open house hosted by the many galleries of primitive art clustered near the Left Bank of the Seine. The French newspaper *Le Monde* gave its exhibits a major review, the author filled with high praise for the sophistication and power of the art but, in equal measure, outraged at the continuing popular identification of this art as "primitive."

He was not the first to see the contradiction in labeling art "primitive" that at its best possesses remarkable aesthetic power and refinement; the problem had been apparent to Parisian artists, critics, and collectors from the time the first masks and figures arrived from Africa late in the 19th century. Picasso spent a weekend at a major exhibition of this "primitive" art in Paris at the Trocadero in 1907; overwhelmed by its powerful directness, he returned to his studio to complete the cubist bodies of *Les Demoiselles d'Avignon* with African-sculpture-inspired heads, and opened a new channel in the then unfolding pathways to modern art.

Several hours by TGV to the south of Paris, this seeming contradiction between "sophistication" and "primitive" is also dramatically apparent in prehistoric cave art. Here in the famous caves of Lascaux, and several more hours away in the Spanish caves of Altamira, our forbears of 15 to 30 thousand years ago painted what is unarguably excellent art—animals quite recognizable, sometimes in groups, in rhythmical and graceful motion. It is reported that on seeing it Picasso proclaimed: "We have invented nothing." Here we are certainly seeing the work of "primitives," yet we are looking at truly remarkable art.

With the transformation of *Les Demoiselles* Picasso was not imitating primitive forms nor was he imitating anything else; possessed of perhaps the best pair of eyes of the 20th century, what he saw and emulated were forms that emerged quite directly from basic mechanisms of the complex machinery by which we see—by which the brain organizes the constant retinal bombardment of photons, the raw materials of perception, into an intelligible world of space and the forms within it. The African art in its bold and simple forms was quite directly responsive to the elementary mechanisms by which the mind begins to comprehend the complex forms around us.

The apparent contradiction between sophisticated art and primitive provenance is resolved when we turn to the first given meaning of the word "primitive" in Webster's Third New International Dictionary: "not derived from or reducible to something else…PRIMARY, ORIGINAL"1 [Capitals in the original].

What does this have to do with Frank Lloyd Wright? A great deal. No Art or artist is an island, and what we learn from one artist elucidates the work of others. What Wright teaches us by his own highly successful discipline is that creation at his high level of achievement is built on the "primitive" or primary form-making processes of perception in a way that makes creation by the architect and re-creation by the viewer extremely efficient and therefore pleasurable. Like the art in the Trocadero that inspired Picasso, his works are truly "primitive" in the sense of being "primary, original," "not derived from... something else"— other than, that is, from the fundamental mechanisms of perception!

ii.

Before continuing, we should distinguish between two aspects of aesthetic experience: the formal and the associational. Our work will deal with the *formal* aspect. By that we mean our responses to formal qualities that do not require prior experience, or a cultural context—they are not "derived from something else." The formal refers to what, without associational reference, the eye and mind make of the photonic mélange that bombards the eye, and our formal aesthetic responses follow from the extent to which those responses are direct, efficient, and pleasing. *Associated* experience—memories, meanings, archetypes—are invoked only after our eyes and mind have done their processing and the forms have emerged; then associations emerge from the purely formal aspects of the experience and merge to form the final complex aesthetic experience. But the two aspects can be separated for purposes of analysis, and must be if we wish to fully understand our experience of art.

Frank Lloyd Wright's works certainly evoke associated experiences, whether those close to elementary instincts like the feeling for shelter, or those linked to our culture or earlier cultures, or, if we believe Carl Jung, those that resonate with deep-seated archetypes. These associations shape and deepen the overall experience, but they are *not* what Wright was referring to when he spoke of the causes of "such vitality, and integrity, and magic as [his buildings] had."[2] He was referring to qualities that constituted an aesthetic signature unique to all his works, regardless of their style or type and various associational resonances. To understand these qualities of "vitality" and "magic" he urged serious students to find in his works the "basic principles" of his "discipline"—to find for themselves the "severe" discipline of "this ideal of internal order, the integration that is organic."[3] These principles and their application we will uncover and demonstrate with case studies in the second, third, and sixth chapters.

iii.

The book has three tasks. The three chapters mentioned above address the first, the discovery of the hidden geometry and its structural laws that are the vehicle of his discipline (which is in fact, as he warned, a "severe" one). In them we will demonstrate case by case how a simple geometry grows and crystallizes according to its internal symmetries to yield beautiful designs. This is architect's work, visual and easy to follow. The role of symmetry is always implicit and, often enough, explicit—and hence its inclusion in the book's title.

The second task is to present a theory as to why the discipline works to yield designs we find beautiful. Here we find help in the fascinating, complex, and uncompleted work of the perceptual sciences. From a comparison of what we know of how the eye and brain process daily experience and what we know of Frank Lloyd Wright's creative method, we will begin to understand how beauty can emerge naturally from the eye's quotidian activity. This is work for scientist and architect working together, and here I must acknowledge my amateur standing in the relevant sciences. But if we are ever to engage in building a bridge between Science and Art, we must communicate between two seemingly very different realms in which very few of us are equally at home. (Although we can hope for that to change. As the bridge-building continues perhaps we can emulate the example of those Renaissance artists equally accomplished as painters and as inventors of their new science of perspective.)

This second task ends, as it must if we are to make any claim to explaining aesthetic experience, with a theory of aesthetics—albeit a partial one. Our theory will merge and resonate with those time-tested theories of art that are based on the belief widely held but generally informally stated (excepting one important instance of mathematical rigor we will discuss): masterpieces emerge from the greatest economy of means effectively employed to create the greatest richness of ends. The theory is physiologically based; it does not depend on the acculturation of the beholder; and it explains the conundrum that greeted me in Paris.

The third task will briefly explore how aesthetic experience connects us to the larger universe in which we find ourselves: Such a connection can hope to carry us beyond art as it is understood today, in the trivialized state to which it has been relegated by the overpowering "reality" of the Newtonian revolution that introduced us to a powerful but hopelessly abstract cosmos of force, mass, and motion. Here we call on what we explored in the second part, namely the symmetries of space, motion, and gravitational force that condition how we experience the world, and examine how these same universal symmetries shape the universe we live in. It is the resonance between our inner laws and the laws governing the greater universe that makes art a pathway to deep and meaningful experience.

iv.

Throughout, there are three goals: first, to elucidate some of Wright's more cryptic written and verbal characterizations of his method; second, to explain the elements of Wright's discipline to such an extent that that it can instruct, discipline, and carry to new levels of achievement the efforts of other architects; and third, to build a bridge between science and the architect's art such that they can inform each the other,...*with the object ever in view,* as Wright's famous mentor, Louis Sullivan, poetically urged,

> *of so humanizing science that it energizes art and so exhibiting the masterful fluency of art that it in turn illuminates science.*[4]

v.

A word of reassurance to those who may be wary of efforts to analyze art, to those inclined to agree with Wordsworth that:

> Our meddling intellect
> Mis-shapes the beauteous forms of things:--
> We murder to dissect.[5]

What the discovery presented in the following pages will *not* do is separate us, except fleetingly, from the immediacy of the lived aesthetic experience which Wright's works so energetically provide. His works will not be beached as if aesthetic corpses on some arid shore, disemboweled by dissection. It should comfort those who cherish direct and deep participation in artistic experience more greatly than they value such analytical knowledge as may be abstracted from it to know that from analysis and discovery much can be learned but nothing of the immediacy and thrill of the aesthetic experience need be lost. Because of the remarkable way in which the mind works, when we are analyzing we can move freely between the hidden geometries we abstract and the enriched experience which follows from their re-mergence into the experience of a flowing and vitally felt complex entity. We can do this because, as has become widely (but perhaps too superficially) known, the brain is bicameral, divided into two hemispheres that overlap in function but which process experience with critical differences in emphases. If the reader will excuse some oversimplification, we can say that that the object is first experienced by the right hemisphere in its time and context and in its wholeness, its *Gestalt.* Then the left hemisphere takes up this experience, pins it down in order to analyze and control, but pays the price of abstracting the experience from its context in the beholder's immediate, lived experience. After being isolated and subjected to analysis by the left hemisphere, the experience can be relinquished and returned to the right hemisphere, enriched as a result. As the classics scholar and psychiatrist Iain McGilchrist describes the process:

> What is offered by the right hemisphere to the left hemisphere is offered back again and taken up into a synthesis involving both hemispheres. This must be true of the processes of creativity, of the understanding of works of art, of the development of the religious sense. In each there is a progress from an intuitive apprehension of whatever it may be, via a more formal process of enrichment through conscious, detailed analytic understanding, to a new, enhanced intuitive understanding of this whole, now transformed by the process that it has undergone.[6]

The movement McGilchrist describes, from right hemisphere to left and returning, at a higher level, back to right again, forms a simple rhythm, in his phrase "an important shape," that for the beholder enriches experience and that for the artist improves creative discipline and facility. This book is conceived somewhat in that shape, as a simple arc that opens as a description of the aesthetic experience of living in a Wright home and continues with analyses of the method that produced it and of the underlying neurobiology of the brain and eye that made it possible. Late in the chapter on science, we will see that our ability to see three-dimensionally deepens our capacity for intense architectural experience, for an "enhanced intuitive understanding of [the] whole."

vi.

It may occur to the reader to ask if Wright himself would have approved of this exercise. I have heard it suggested that Wright, like medieval artisans, kept his methods secret so as to deter successful competition. I don't believe that. The reason for his seemingly cryptic, unsystematic way of talking about his "severe discipline" I think has more to do with the young age (10 years) at which he was introduced to the illuminating geometries of the Froebel system, and to which he then devoted several happy years.[7] His youthful mastery of Froebel's teachings laid the foundations of his later method. His "basic principles" may have become so innate so early on that, in his maturity, designs crystallized around them, final in dress and detail, with little conscious attention required by the designer to their unclothed origins. To reverse the flow of mental activity in order to abstract basic principles (which he probably regarded as self-evident anyway) from a cauldron of intense, highly synthesizing activity for which they are the foundation, would have been an unnatural and laborious act.

He left it to some of us less favored by early circumstance and talent to do this upstream (i.e., analytical) work. We begin here, exploring beneath the flow of seductively rich surfaces and effects of Wright's works to uncover core principles that produced them, our efforts made both pleasurable and frustrating by the beguiling harmonies of the subject, but well-rewarded by the elegant simplicity and obvious heuristic value of the underlying patterns they uncover.

As we look to the science that explains how from these principles Wright created his serene harmonies of space and form, we begin to understand that the Froebel geometries trained the eye and mind not so much in the order of nature, as Wright and Froebel believed, as it did in the fundamental forms and mechanisms of our visual apparatus, the inner workings of mind and eye, that, as research since their time has begun to reveal, shape the dynamics of visual perception. Wright probably would have embraced this science, had it been in place. Ralph Waldo Emerson, a philosopher he favored, had written: "For the truth was in us before it was reflected to us from natural objects."[8]

"The truth [that] was in us" to which Emerson referred, when stripped of mystical connotations, science would say are those mechanisms that allow us to intelligibly apprehend the forms "reflected…from natural objects." Current theories suggests that these mechanisms at their most fundamental are simple and favor simple symmetries. When orchestrated in a manner consistent with their inner structure, I will argue, they are capable of producing objects of great beauty. If we assume, not unreasonably, that these mechanisms are "of the fiber of our own nature," then Wright, writing in 1910, may have adumbrated knowledge to be delivered many decades later by scientists probing the mysteries of perception when with insight and uncharacteristic circumspection he asserted:

> … if and when we perceive anything to be beautiful...this means that a glimpse of something essentially of the fiber of our own inner nature is revealed to us. Through his own deeper insight the artist shares with us this revelation…We have a vision of innate harmony not fully understood by us today, though perhaps to be appreciated tomorrow.[9]

Wright knew he was that artist. His "tomorrow" is our "today," and our findings and the science that supports them now give further evidence and concrete representation for what Emerson intuited and to which he gave form.

1
THE SEARCH

THE JOHN HAYNES HOUSE
1951, FORT WAYNE, INDIANA

In the fall of 1972, I moved into the John Haynes house, the one Frank Lloyd Wright work in my hometown of Fort Wayne, Indiana. This move narrowed, for the final time, my search for the secrets of the master architect whose works I had first sought to emulate during my architectural schooling at Yale. Natural and professional habits of constant visual analysis now could feast, daily; all my senses would be absorbed in an enveloping, uniquely integrated aesthetic experience—whose impact I could not foretell.

ENTRY and GALLERY
LOOKING EAST

The home is a very representative example of the Usonian type, designed in 1951, 15 years into the evolution of that style. At 1,340 usable square feet it is small even by Usonian standards, but well made of some of the best Usonian materials and details. It incorporates a combination of wood shingle hip roofs (employing, not uncharacteristically for a Usonian, asymmetrical roof slopes) and a flat carport roof; brick exterior walls of beautiful burgundy and tan hues; and Tidewater red cypress for all interior surfaces not of brick, milled to be joined by tongue and groove on the ceilings, by board and batten on the walls.

To live in a Wright home is to live in an all-encompassing "School of Frank Lloyd Wright." I awoke every morning in one of its classrooms. My first waking experiences were of the projecting ceiling ledges that capped the built-in wardrobes and intersected neatly with the cathedral ceiling; of the shelves and the built-in desk whose horizontal trim flowed with perfect alignment into the battens of the board and batten walls; and of the narrow band of rhythmically patterned windows high along the otherwise closed street-side wall. All of this complemented by brass hardware: simple round brass closet pulls, continuous brass piano hinges on the wardrobe doors and folding partitions (a surprisingly effective way of highlighting certain complementary verticals), and brass screws, evenly spaced, fastening the battens to the boards (with the screwdriver slots left precisely horizontal, if the carpenter had done his work right). To control cracking, the brick-red concrete floor was incised with the 4-ft. by 4-ft.-square design module, rather literally underscoring the design's formal origin in a four-foot grid system. The total effect reminded me of sailing yachts of a certain size: compact but extremely efficient, designed for maximum economy of use and ease of movement. One was left with a feeling of comfort and sufficiency, and because of the constant flow of lines and planes into each other, even of expansiveness.

LIVING ROOM,
LOOKING WEST

The warmth and flow created by the neat fit and supple interactions of the rich materials carried through the house, culminating in the remarkable living room. Small but seemingly spacious, with spaces flowing outward from it onto the terrace, into the dining area, and down the long bedroom wing gallery and into the master bedroom, it was the center of a complex of spaces inviting the eye to constantly move outward but constantly to return, generating, finally, a serene resting place that breathed tranquility and felt secure, leaving one with a feeling of repose.

From the outside, the thorough articulation of functions into separate wings and subordinate masses resulted in a plan that spread out into the site in three directions. From the street one saw several enclosing masses, crisply defined by the handsome brick: a long, low bedroom wing, its flow eastward accentuated by a patterned ribbon-window along most of its length, met at its west end by the kitchen wing that thrust forward toward the street, its movement paced by four equally spaced, vertical slit windows—accents to a well sheltered entrance. Mediated by a third, smaller mass (enclosing a front bathroom), their intersection was accentuated by the loftiest element of the house, a large square brick surround enclosing a kitchen skylight and fireplace chimney. From this enclosure the living room wing thrust westward, shorter and higher than the bedroom wing and counterbalancing its eastward thrust; and a flat carport roof thrust toward the street and across the circular drive, to be anchored at its outer end by a brick tool shed. Prominent wood-shingled hip roofs dominated the bedroom and living room wings, and their strongly cantilevered ends hovered above and emphasized the flat crest of the gentle rise (to one of the high points in a fairly flat city) on which it sat.

The high skylight enclosure, rising slightly above the roofline, created a pyramidal massing that gave strong anchorage and a sense of stability and rootedness; and yet the wings thrusting outward, strongly accentuated by their emphatically cantilevered roofs, made the home appear to be constantly reaching out, filled with energy, poised for action. All this vitality in a diminutive structure almost involuntarily inspired a theriomorphic image, although one of relatively modest character. I saw it as a frog prince of the Usonians, constantly alert on its lily-pad and poised to strike. (Perhaps an appropriate response to a home that began life as one of Wright's self-named "polliwog plans"!)

There was in final effect an equipoise of opposites so often found in Wright's works: an ineffable but palpable constant tension between two seemingly incompatible qualities—constant motion and serenity. Despite their energy, interior and exterior alike embodied the quality Wright valued above almost all others: the quality, as he stated it, of "repose [so that a work would be] in absolute poise, leaving nothing but a feeling of quiet satisfaction with its sense of completeness."[10] But it was clear that the carefully chosen materials, sheltering roofs, flowing lines, and fine detailing were not the direct cause of this repose and certainly not of the home's essential dynamism. They were merely the means of expressing some underlying order that produced these qualities. With respect to this unknown order, Wright himself was cryptic: "repose" was the "reward of integrity," he had written, and it followed from "the discipline of...the ideal of internal order, the integration that is organic."[11] But what was this "internal order," and what "discipline" produced it? The house remained the constant reminder of these questions, but the unyielding guardian of the answers.

FALSE STARTS

Scholars of Wright's work have thoroughly explored and explained several layers of his complex and multi-layered creations: March and Steadman's topological studies, which show the remarkable topological equivalence of geometrically very different Usonian floor plans; William Storrer's systematic typology of the Usonians and history of the grid system, included in his heroic cataloging of all of Wright's built works; the helpful studies on Wright's approach to spatial organization gathered into one volume by Robert McCarter, including McCarter's own insightful scholarship and unerring taste; the penetrating insights of Neil Levine; and the writings and lectures of Vincent Scully, my professor at Yale, whose historical erudition enabled him to relate Wright's achievements to the currents of his own and of earlier times. But in none of these were there attempts to trace the specific geometry of the "discipline" and its "basic principles" to which Mr. Wright credited much of his success.

Nor during my first otherwise happy years did my Usonian offer up its secrets. Certainly they did not lie on the surface, felicitous as it was. The warmth and harmony of materials, the careful joining and fit that created flowing continuities, the deeply extending roofs that carried the sheltering comfort of overhead protection beyond the enclosing walls—all were critical to the experience of the house, but none explained its improbable combination of a sense of constant movement with a feeling of rootedness and repose. What would? What was the source of its great orderliness and calm, in spite of its seemingly total freedom from formal constraints?

Organizing and proportioning methods employed by great architects before and during his time were not the answer. The Golden Section and its elegant permutations were seldom found, nor was its numerical counterpart, the Fibonacci series.[12] Even had they been, it is unlikely that they would have been the generators of his governing "internal order": the Golden Section had been used intuitively by artists for centuries, and, in modern times, by Le Corbusier, who employed it in its geometrical form to set proportions and in its numerical form to generate his proportioning system, *The Modular*; but it was always used to refine a predetermined form rather than to generate one *de novo*.

Likewise, parallel or orthogonal "regulating lines", whose effective use Le Corbusier illustrates in *Towards a New Architecture*, primarily have been employed, as he wrote, to "rectify, correct, give point to and pull together"[13] forms whose basic order has already been established. He convincingly demonstrates the critical role of "the placement of the right angle" in producing the powerful drama of Michelangelo's Capitol, the elegant poise of the Petit Trianon at Versailles, and the clarity of his own houses in Auteuil; but in each case, he wrote: "The regulating process, based on a geometric equilibrium, thus merely orders, clarifies, and purifies a design that has already been drawn up."[14]

1.1. THE PETIT TRIANON, VERSAILLES

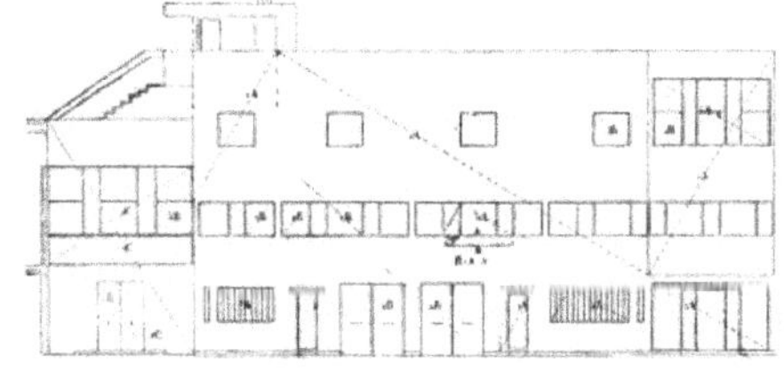

1.2. THE CAPITOL, ROME

1.3. LE CORBUSIER AND PIERRE JEANNERET, 1924 TWO HOUSES AT AUTEUIL

NARROWING the SEARCH

Unlike Le Corbusier's examples, the primary source of aesthetic power in Wright's designs is to be found not in their well-designed façades, but in the plans from which the buildings emerged. It is possible to experience the plans themselves as fresh and alive, and as capable as their three-dimensional progeny of revealing the powerful thrust and balance of masses and cantilevered planes. (The plans, of course, include by dotted outline all overhead ceilings, roofs, and clerestories, and thus present all three dimensions of their buildings.) Wright himself encouraged us to recognize the expressive power of his plans, and to respect their dominant role in the designs:

> A good plan is the beginning and the end…its development in all directions is inherent – inevitable… There is more beauty in a fine ground plan than in almost any of its ultimate consequences. … Were all elevations of the genuine buildings of the world lost and the ground plans saved, each building would construct itself again.[15]

For one tempted to doubt the importance of the plan in the design process, there is the testimony of an eye witness, his apprentice Barry Byrne:

> Although Mr. Wright is sometimes pictured as studying his compositions in perspective, this was not his way when I worked under him. The designs he made existed primarily in those greatest of his contributions to a living architecture, his incomparable building plans. The value of his exterior massing and details derived from their appearance of inevitability and from the fact of their indisputable rightness as expressions of the plan. Endowed as he was with an unerring sense of the third dimension, Mr. Wright…always arrived at his designs in plan and elevation.[16]

Accordingly, I focused on his plans, and, as I narrowed my search, focused more specifically on the plans of his late "Usonian style." These latter encompassed an astonishing variety of formal types and building techniques and, coming late in his career, were the flowering of fully matured genius. Unlike the earlier Prairie Style homes, their profusion of forms and formal invention hid all traces of the formal symmetries that had been the backbone of most traditional styles—which meant there was less danger that conventional or frequently repeated forms or effects would be incorrectly generalized as his "basic principles." Taken together the Usonians constituted the perfect hunting ground for explanations that lay beneath the surface.

REGULATING LINES

Efforts to find "regulating lines" in Wright's plans yielded little; those that were found hinted at a wealth of harmonizing relationships but did not illuminate a process or generative principles. For examples, look at my analysis by regulating lines of the Herbert Jacobs house, and Robert McCarter's :

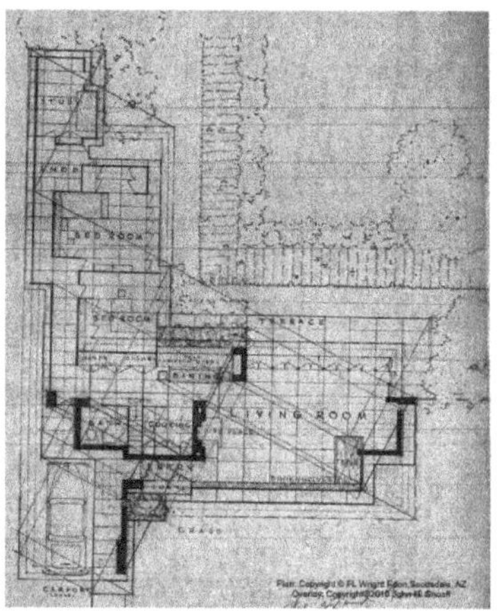

MY ANALYSIS

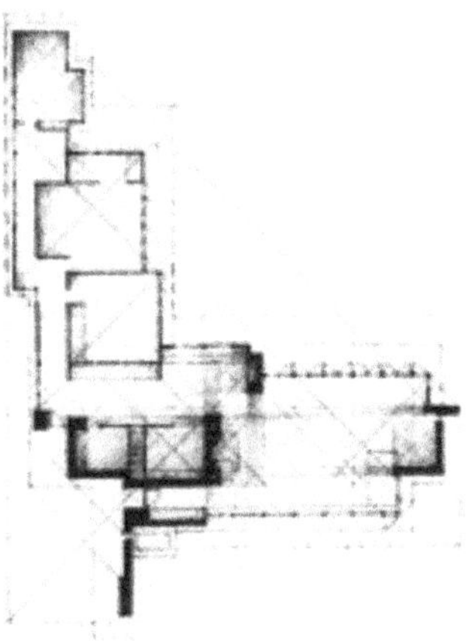

1.4. ROBERT MCCARTER'S ANALYSIS

Neither offers much clarification, although McCarter strikes closer to the essential truth in that his regulating lines hint at a wealth of hidden squares—and squares turned out to be, as we shall see, the basic building blocks of the design.

The SQUARE has long been an important organizer, usually hidden, of the façades ("elevations," as architects call them) of architectural masterpieces.

The SQUARE

Le Corbusier found, or came close to finding, the square as the primary compositional device behind the façades of two masterpieces of his adopted Paris: the great Cathedral of Notre Dame and François Blondel's Porte Saint-Denis.

1.5. NOTRE DAME,
LE CORBUSIER'S ANALYSIS

1.6. NOTRE DAME,
ANOTHER WAY OF LOOKING AT
LE CORBUSIER'S ANALYSIS

Let's look at Notre Dame: Le Corbusier presents it as being proportioned by intersecting arcs of circles (on the left, in black); but the arc of each quarter circle defines a square, and so Notre Dame also can be seen as proportioned by squares, three high and two wide. Against this stable background the rose window at the center of the façade is enclosed by a seventh square centered vertically on the primary squares and resting neatly on the top horizontal edge shared by the two squares at the base. The whole composition provides a clear, simple, and strong framework for the rhythmic play of Gothic tracery and sculpture.

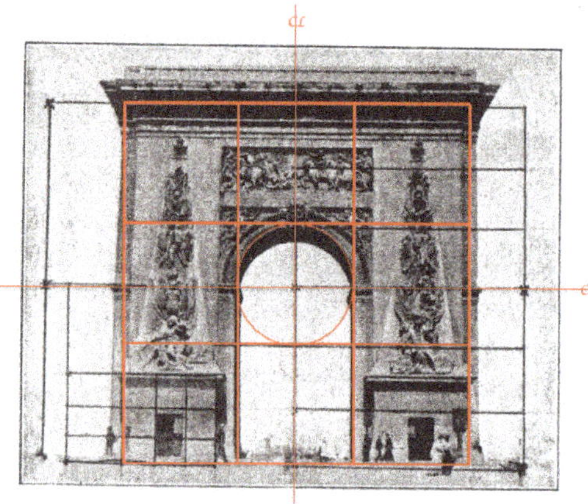

1.7. THE PORTE SAINTE-DENIS

THE ENCOMPASSING SQUARE TRISECTED

1.8. THE PORTE SAINT-DENIS

THE PILASTERS RELATE THE MAJOR SQUARE. TO A CENTRAL DOUBLE-SQUARE

We turn now to The Porte Saint-Denis., a fine work by the 17th-century architect, Nicholas François Blondel. Le Corbusier, extracting from the architect's notes, writes "A bold regulating line, on the unit of 3, divides the ensemble of the arch, and the various other parts of the work, as to height and breadth, and governs everything according to the same rule of 3."[17]

If we look past the rather cryptic diagram Le Corbusier laid over Blondel's arch (the black lines), analysis reveals both a great simplicity and a great subtlety. The great simplicity is the square which circumscribes the whole composition and its trisection vertically and horizontally (to which Blondel presumably refers). The trisection creates a smaller central square that centers and circumscribes precisely the semicircular arch.

The subtlety is found in the handling of the flanking pilasters. Their outer edges coincide with the great square while their inner edges coincide with a vertical double-square; thus they mediate between these two simple geometric forms — they attract the eye to both of these primary forms and lead it back and forth between them—giving life to an otherwise potentially inert composition.

1.9. THE HIGH COURT AT CHANDIGARH

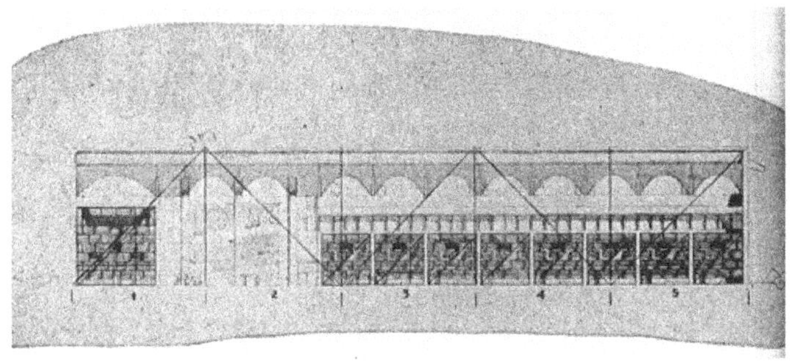

1.10. THE HIGH COURT AT CHANDIGARH

ELEVATION

Some twenty-five years after publishing these examples, Le Corbusier used multiple squares to compose a work far more powerful than his homes in Auteuil: the Palace of Justice in Chandigarh. In *Modular 2* he presents its elevation as being enclosed within a five-square rectangle, and shows that its beautifully patterned *brises-soleils* are framed within a series of subordinate squares. The inclusion of the diagonals in his presentation of the five squares demonstrates that he had not abandoned one of his earlier compositional tools, "the placement of the right angle." Here the right angles formed at the meetings of the diagonals of adjacent squares reinforce the strong structural relationships already established by the squares' common horizontal axis.

The PLAN

In virtually all of Wright's orthogonal-grid-based works, the simple square—the form he had mastered in childhood—emerges from a grid of squares or double-squares to generate the plan; multiplied, rescaled, combined at various scales and overlapping patterns, the squares generate a complete composition. Unlike architects before him whose visions came into focus in the elevation, as Le Corbusier's examples demonstrate, for Wright, the plan, not the elevation, has most control over the design; when a plan is generated on an orthogonal grid, the square not merely corrects or refines; it unleashes its protean symmetries to guide the design's unfolding.

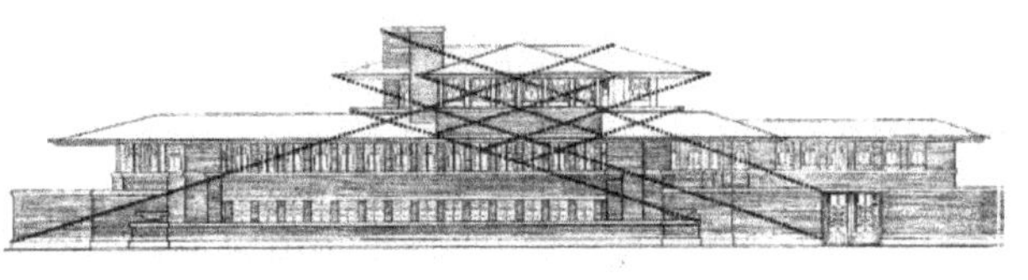

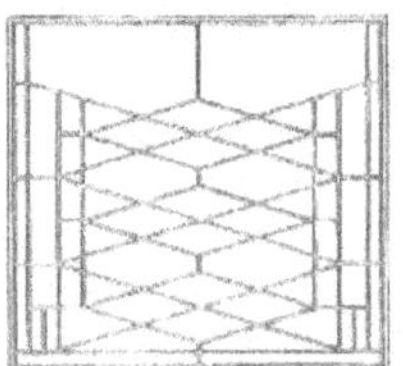

1.11. THE ROBIE HOUSE
PRIMARY WINDOW DESIGN ELEMENTS ARE PARALLEL TO THE ROOF SLOPES

Even though his elevations are handsome, and some clearly have been refined by the deliberate use of regulating lines—as in the correspondence between window design and roof slopes of the Robie house shown here—they give only a pale hint of the true character and impact of the buildings, which typically are dramas written in three dimensions.

The plans tell much more: the plans in themselves possess that astonishing equipoise between a sense of constant energy and movement and a quality of balance and repose that is manifest in so many of his works. Wright truly believed "a good plan is the beginning and the end."[18] The presentation of the Robie house shown below, done by an apprentice some years after the home was built, graphically asserts the drama of the work rising in its three-dimensional glory, firmly rooted but thrusting powerfully, from a two-dimensional plan. A little to the apprentice's surprise "the stark graphic black-on-white presentation did not produce a two-dimensional effect, [but] rather emphasized the depth of his poetry and the power of the third dimension."[19]

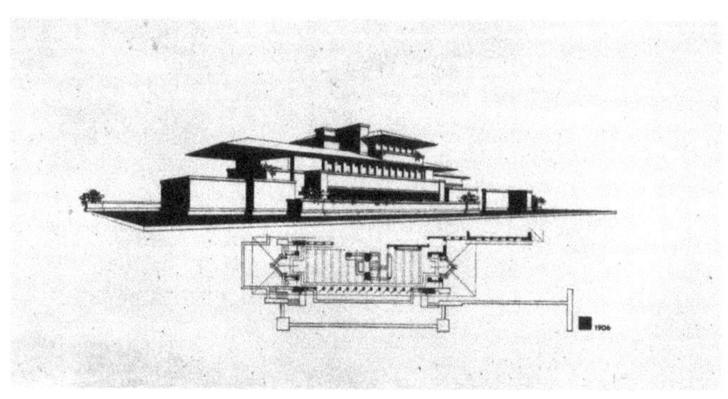

1.12. THE ROBIE HOUSE 1906
PRESENTATION DRAWING OF PERSPECTIVE AND PLAN.

The GRID

An understanding of Wright's plans begins with an appreciation of the unit system on which they are based. Almost every plan was developed over a grid of identical units. Usually it was the square, although often in the Usonians he used the double-square, and later in his career, the equilateral triangle and its kin, the rhombus and the hexagon. In 1925 he wrote:

> All the buildings I have ever built, large and small, are fabricated upon a unit system—as the pile of a rug is stitched into the warp. Thus each structure is an ordered fabric. Rhythm, consistent scale of parts, and an economy of construction are greatly facilitated by this simple expedient—a mechanical one absorbed in a final result to which all has given more consistent texture, a more tenuous quality as a whole.[20]

He carefully chose the scale of the grid unit most suitable to the scale and character of the project. But the discipline of a grid by itself did not guarantee good design; of itself it would not have prevented bland, diffuse, and inert results (as the efforts of others have too often proved). The controlling influence of a square grid did not begin to explain that characteristically Wrightian combination of vitality and serenity that I found in the plan and in my daily experience in the Haynes House, to which we will now return.

2
DISCOVERY: An IMAGE in FOUR DIMENSIONS

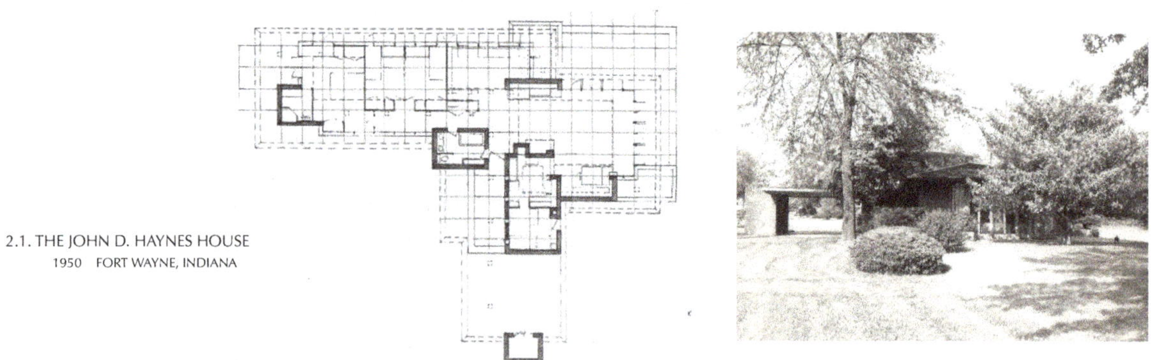

2.1. THE JOHN D. HAYNES HOUSE
1950 FORT WAYNE, INDIANA

Although the house yielded its secrets reluctantly, after the first clues emerged others quickly followed. After haphazard and frustrating months of futile probing, late in an evening spent staring at the plan, all previous theories receding, my mind a blank, a pattern suddenly detached itself from the comfortable homogeneity of the grid lines crisscrossing the living area: two squares, one nested inside the other and the two symmetrical about a common vertical axis, jumped off the page to define the rigorous symmetry of a living space that heretofore had seemed a casual nexus of intersecting spaces. The smaller square, four units on a side, coincided with the two window walls and the face of the dining alcove; the larger square, eight units on a side, inscribed the perimeter of the terrace and its flanking planters. (2.1.A.)

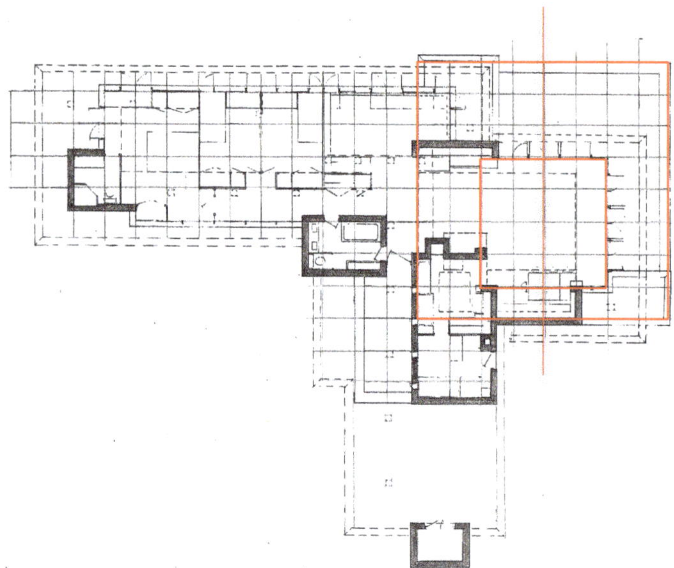

2.1..A.
A PAIR OF SQUARES, BILATERALLY SYMMETRICAL ABOUT A VERTICAL AXIS, ANCHOR THE DESIGN.

Following this modest but startling insight, a deeper understanding of the rest of the plan rapidly unfolded. Exploration with triangle and T-square revealed that from these two squares one could generate the two wings. Duplicating the 4-unit square to the left, sliding it upward by one-half its height, and finally tripling it to make a 3-square run, the triplet formed the bedroom wing. (2.1.B.) A 2½ unit square at the lower left corner of the 8-unit square and generated about its diagonal, when repeated once upward and tripled downward, became a run of five squares that formed the vertical wing: the top three squares linked the entry area, kitchen and utility room, and the bottom two located and anchored the tool shed at the end of the carport. (2.1.B.)

So far all these forms conformed to the unit lines. In the case of the thicker brick walls, one face or the other coincided with a unit line or ½ unit line. The choice of which face, however, was not arbitrary: for the left and bottom walls of the utility room, the interior face coincided with a unit line, and when the square of which they were constituent was expanded along its diagonal it generated a new, slightly larger square that circumscribed the exterior face of the brick walls. When this new square was tripled, the new triad precisely circumscribed the mass of the vertical wing, and a fourth identical square at the upper end of the sequence outlined the upper planter. As if an echo, a smaller triad circumscribed the tool shed and tied it to the main structure. (2.1. C.)

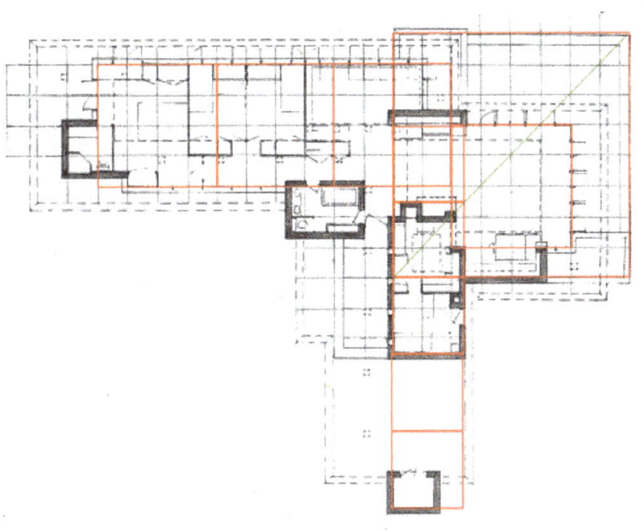

2.1. B.
SQUARES ARE MULTIPLIED, OR ARE DIMINISHED AND THEN MULTIPLIED, TO FORM THE TWO WINGS

When the bedroom wing triad is shifted one unit to the left, the left end that previously defined the corner of the master bedroom now fixes the end of the master bathroom, and the right square of the triad now neatly defines the corner of the music alcove. (2.1. C.)

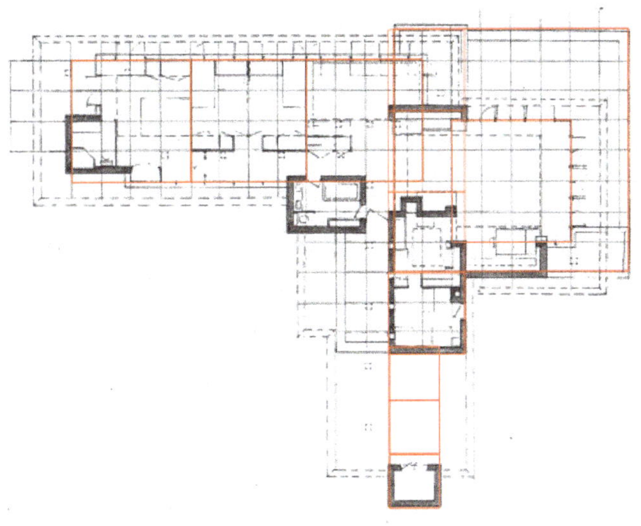

2.1. C.
SHIFTS IN RUNS AND RESCALING OF SQUARES FURTHER DEFINE THE PLAN.

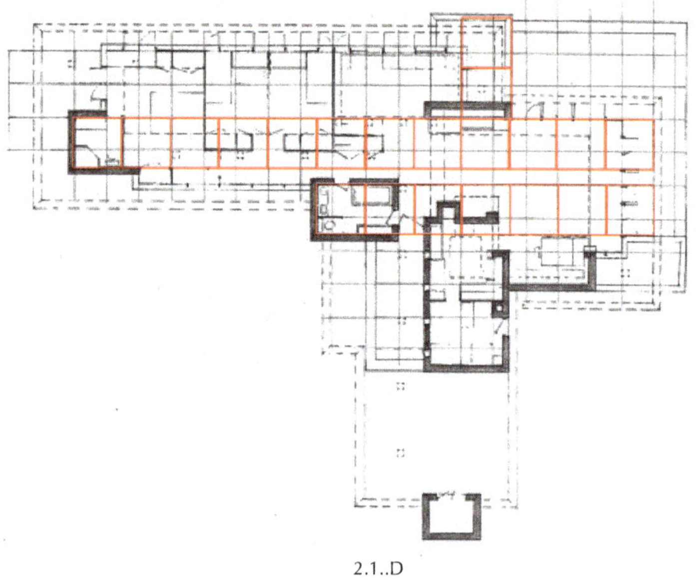

2.1..D

SMALL TERMINAL MASSES INTEGRATED BY PARALLEL RUNS OF SQUARES.

Two brick masses remained to be integrated, those defining the master and front bathrooms. Both were 1½ units wide, as measured between interior faces, and these faces coincided with grid and ½ grid lines. Both terminated implicit linear horizontal runs of 1½ unit squares, one run aligned with the master bathroom and continued by the living-area glass wall and the face of the alcove shelf, the other generated by the front bathroom and completed by one face of the rightmost planter. These two runs ran parallel to each other and terminated together at the inner edge (the edge that is most frequently seen from inside the house) of the roof fascia. (2.1. D.)

Finally, the roof revealed itself to be defined by multiple squares. Two large squares coincide with the outer edges of the fasciae of the long hip roof over the bedroom wing. One diagonal of the rightmost square is shown; it forms a right angle with a long fixed diagonal that goes down and to the right, coinciding with one of the two diagonals of a large square, three sides of which outline the living area roof. (Recall the importance Le Corbusier attached to "the placement of the right angle": Wright has used it here to "lock" together the bedroom and living-room roofs.) (2.1.E.)

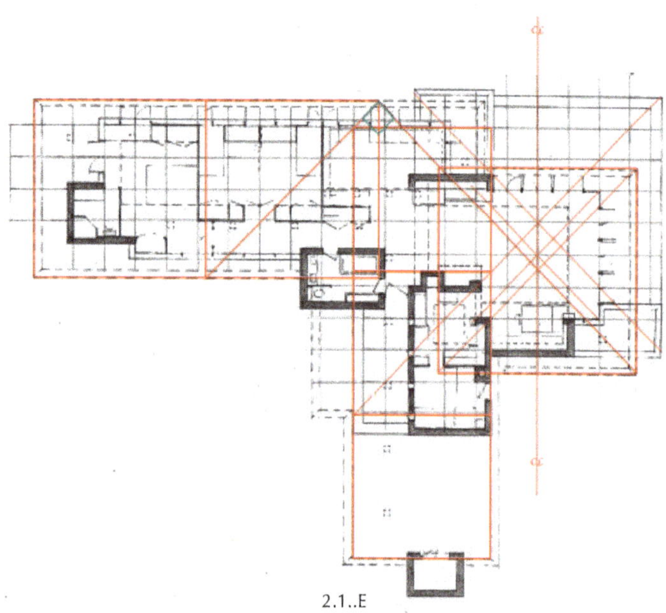

2.1..E

THE ROOFS ARE INTEGRATED BY LINKED SQUARES.

The carport roof is shaped by a triad of squares 4½ units on a side that run from the tool shed up to the back wall of the bedroom wing. One diagonal of the middle of these squares coincides with one of the diagonals of the 8-unit square originally identified as one of the two squares defining the living area. (2.1.E)

All this seemed sound and satisfactory. But at the time I appreciated neither its true significance nor its broader applicability. I was not yet prepared or equipped to realize these patterns were the products of a dynamic process, of the geometry and by the eye; nor did I understand that the aesthetic experience generated by the resulting patterns was itself dynamic, recapitulating the dynamics by which they were created. Only some years later, when struggling with the challenge of designing a summer home for my brother, did I recognize the value of what I had uncovered. A simple change in the home's interior geometry (which, being a good disciple, I was developing on a grid) suddenly changed something mediocre into something fairly good. Almost accidentally, I had caused the repetition of a simple pattern that carried through the house, which, although hidden, suddenly gave the design clarity and a pleasing aspect. The insight was really no more than a recapitulation of what had already been uncovered in the Haynes plan, but this time it resonated with portents of a greater significance. Spontaneously I heard myself saying, "So this is what Frank Lloyd Wright was doing all along."

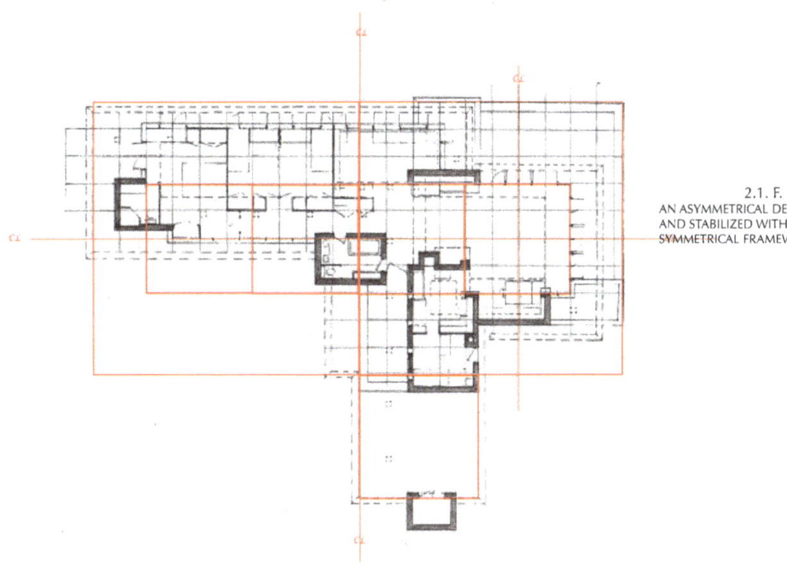

2.1. F.
AN ASYMMETRICAL DESIGN BALANCED AND STABILIZED WITHIN A BILATERALLY SYMMETRICAL FRAMEWORK.

Revelation in hand, I went back to the Haynes house analysis, memorialized on now-yellowing paper. It remained sound, but was now resonant with meaning. In re-analysis, a fresh surprise unfolded: the large 8-unit square encompassing the living room, when expanded along one diagonal, formed a 10-unit square when doubled to the left formed a double-square encompassing the entire hip roof and the terrace. One additional, 4½ unit square circumscribed the remainder of the carport roof. The vertical centerline of this double-square coincided with the continuous line formed by the outer edge of the entry porch and the fascia of the carport —entrance roof. The horizontal centerline of this encompassing double-square was also the centerline of the 4-unit square that defines the heart of the living room, and this square was the rightmost in a four-square run that defined the length of the house and was placed symmetrically within the encompassing double-square, a placement that gave stable anchorage to an active composition. Thus he had generated an asymmetrical design, albeit one beautifully balanced, unexpectedly laid out within a bilaterally symmetrical enclosure with a strongly expressed centerline of (2.1. F.)

(A strong desire to emphasize the vertical centerline may be the reason Wright cantilevered the carport roof far to the left—so precariously far that the builder may have balked. As John Haynes recounted to me many years later, there was a visit to Taliesin, at which the builder, a feisty fellow not at all intimidated by the great man, said, "The building won't work this way." Mr. Wright said, "My buildings always work." Builder and architect put their heads together and quickly reconciled. We have no direct evidence that the cantilever was the issue—the three principals are no longer with us—but the house was built with the roof shifted to the right four feet and centered on the tool shed, as is now shown on William Storrer's "as built" plan in *The Frank Lloyd Wright Companion*— and that is the only visible change to the construction plan that came from Wright's office, and from which the plan shown here is traced.)

To summarize: an asymmetrical plan was placed neatly within a highly symmetrical double square, a plan almost all of which was generated, coordinated, and unified by manipulations of squares. The squares grow or diminish, bilaterally symmetrical about both orthogonal and diagonal axes, by unit or ½ unit multiples; and they multiply, usually along an axis. One simple form, the triple-square, is repeated at several scales, giving rhythm and coherence to the whole. Some simple forms overlap, and each contributes its particular quality to the final experience. The bilaterally symmetrical nesting of the large living room squares, for example, contributes stability, and the linear runs of the wings generate movement. The whole is placed within a bilaterally symmetrical framework, and the strong emphasis on its central axis stabilizes and anchors this otherwise seemingly free and asymmetrical design.

VERTICAL UNITS

All dimensions in the plan were now accounted for, but what about vertical dimensions—did Wright have a unit system for them as well? He did: his unit for vertical dimensions was set by the modular dimensions of the building materials. The unit used in the Haynes house was one that had become a Usonian standard —1'-1"—the height of a board and batten, dictated by the board and batten construction of all the interior walls. Repetition of these vertical units gave a pleasing harmony and rhythm to the elevations and clarity to the plan-generated three-dimensional dynamics. The vertical module for the brick exterior walls, 8" of height for three brick courses, no matter how multiplied, didn't match any multiple of 1'-1". But Wright adjusted the ceiling height of his lowest spaces (which occurred along the galleries) upward to 6'-8" from the 6'-6" produced by three multiples of the board and batten module, and this corresponds to an exact multiple of 8".

The DISCIPLINE

These fresh insights into the Haynes house prompted the obvious question, to what extent would they apply to Wright's other designs? Testing of other plans followed. Cautious at first, I began with explorations of Usonians that, like the Haynes House, had plans based on orthogonal grids. Thirty some analyses later, it was clear that without exception, *all* the plans grew from a basic square, varied in size but generally of whole or one-half multiples of the basic grid unit. Analysis of designs from the earlier Prairie-style period, including some with no grid shown, yielded the same result. Whether Prairie or Usonian, it was apparent that the clarity and vitality of even the simplest designs had depended on something more than straightforward adherence to a grid and the use of simple forms. That "something" turned out to be multiple hidden, overlapping, and interacting square-based patterns that the eye repetitively traced, cycled, and integrated into vivid and lively yet stable images.

Wright's discipline begins with the plan, and the plan begins with a grid. As he had written, "All the buildings I have built—large and small—are fabricated upon a unit system,"[21] the "unit" being a square, hexagon, or triangle; the "system" being the grid of units from which the unit arose. In all of his plans one or more units of the grid emerge from the grid, then multiply, or grow by unit or half-unit increments, forming simple shapes which overlap and interact, each shape retaining its integrity while interweaving with the others to form a well-integrated symphony, one often rich and complex. He gratefully credits the origins of his method to Frederick Froebel's kindergarten blocks and grid—this much is well-known—but in the full flowering of his maturity the integration of patterns of similar shapes at different scales, overlapping and interacting in conformity with their internal axial structures, goes far beyond the capabilities of Froebel's system.

This process of integration requires a duration of time to unfold—*not only in creation, but in its beholding. Time becomes a dimension of the aesthetic image along with the three spatial ones.* Later we will explore this time-dependency of our perceptions, which *only appear* to be instantaneous. For now, with respect to the analyses before us, it is important to know that this time-dependency generates a dynamism which explains certain aesthetic characteristics of Wright's works. (It also is the reason the case studies present underlying patterns—the red outlines—separately, rather than overlapping them in one drawing; each retains its integrity and is experienced separately, but constantly recycles with the others to form a dynamic yet coherent image that merges only in the fourth dimension.) We will now look at his method at work.

3
THREE CASE STUDIES

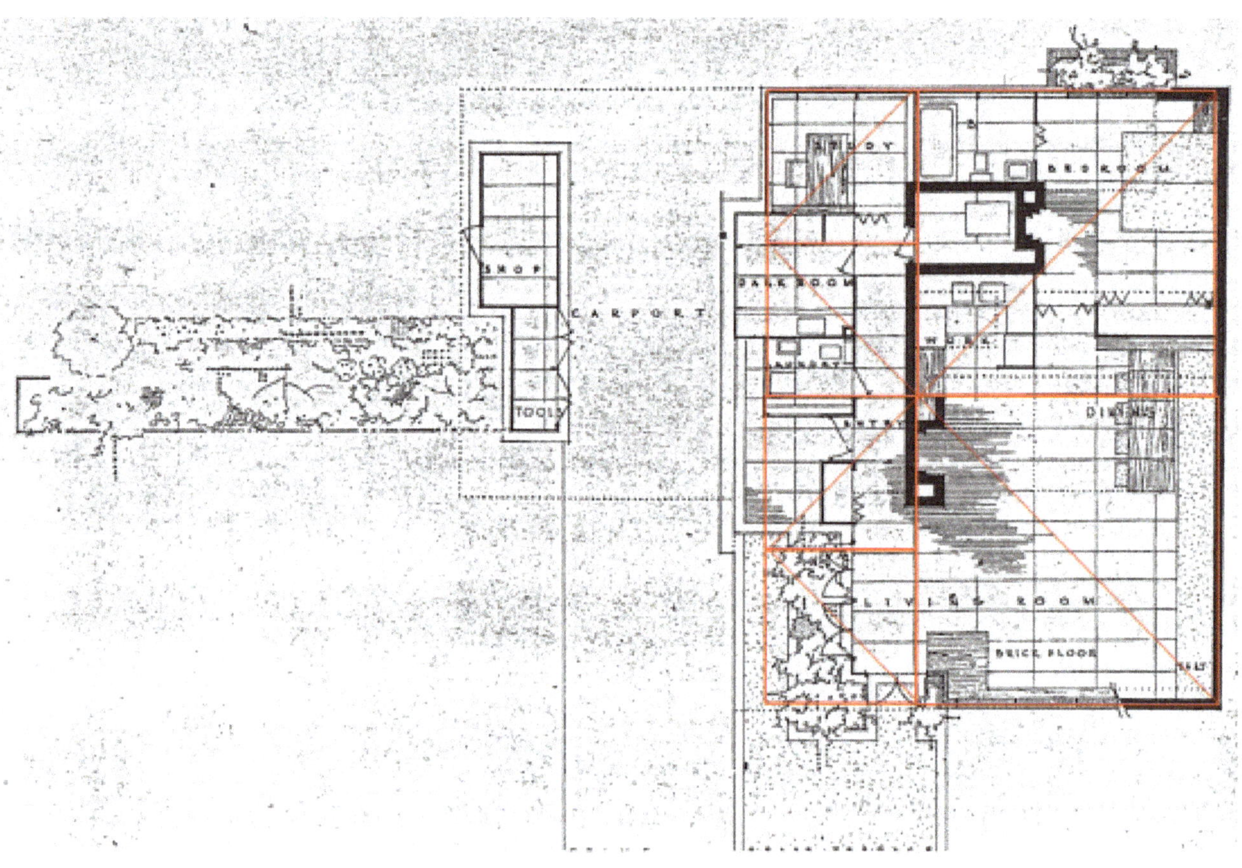

Let us look at the deceptively simple ROY E. PETERSEN HOUSE. It is designed as a Usonian five years after the the advent of the style. The residence is a disarmingly modest lakeshore home whose floor plan lies within a simple rectangle. In spite of its simplicity the plan lures us in: the eye is drawn into the house and from room to room, to elements unremarkable in themselves but neatly related to each other. In counterpoint to the invitation inward, a lanai and a garden strip reach outward into a site to which the house lays claim with quiet authority. There is no obvious reason for the plan's appealing qualities, but discovery of a simple underlying geometry begins to give us clues.

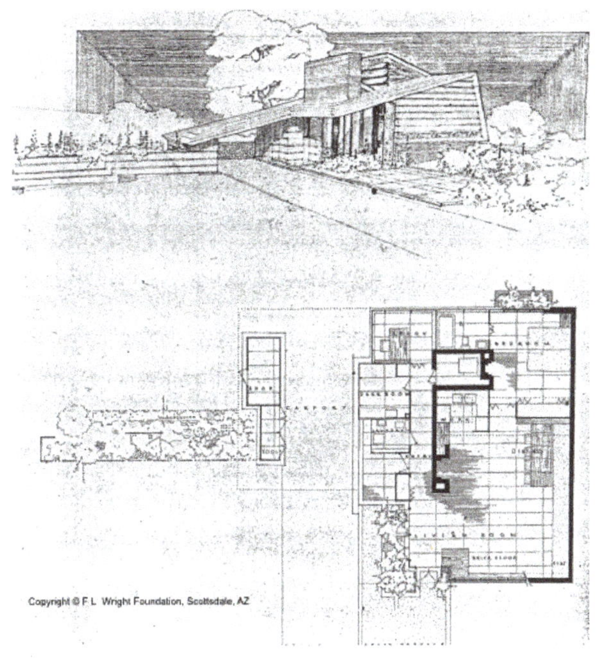

3.1.. ROY E. PETERSEN HOUSE
1941, RACINE, WISCONSIN

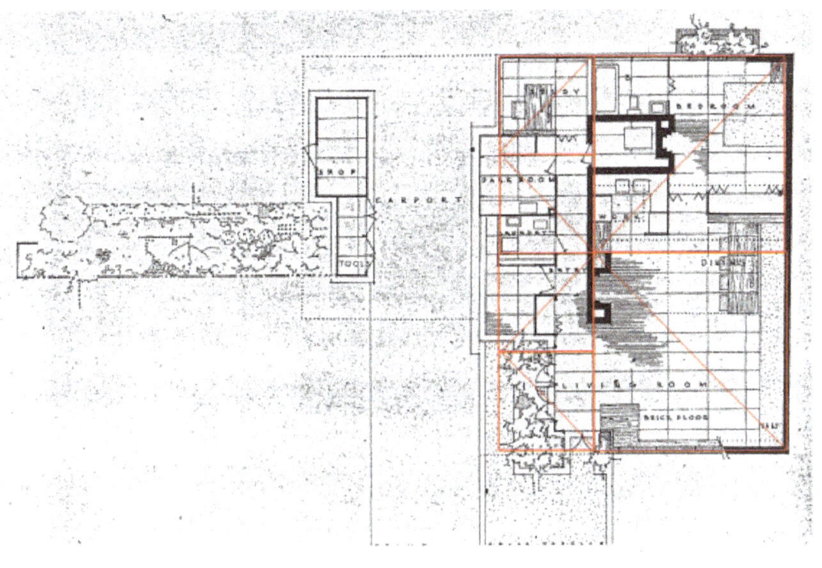

3.1..A.
DOUBLE SQUARES DETERMINE THE PLAN

The plan, we discover, is generated by patterns of double-squares and rows of squares, interlocked by shared diagonals, all lying hidden beneath the surface. We can begin with the long masonry wall that divides the interior vertically. To its right, the larger spaces are contained within a large double-square, five units wide by ten high (for 1-by-2 grids, we call the long side one unit and the short side one-half unit); to the left, the remainder is circumscribed by four squares (two double-squares) each $2^1/_2$ units on a side. (3.1.A.)

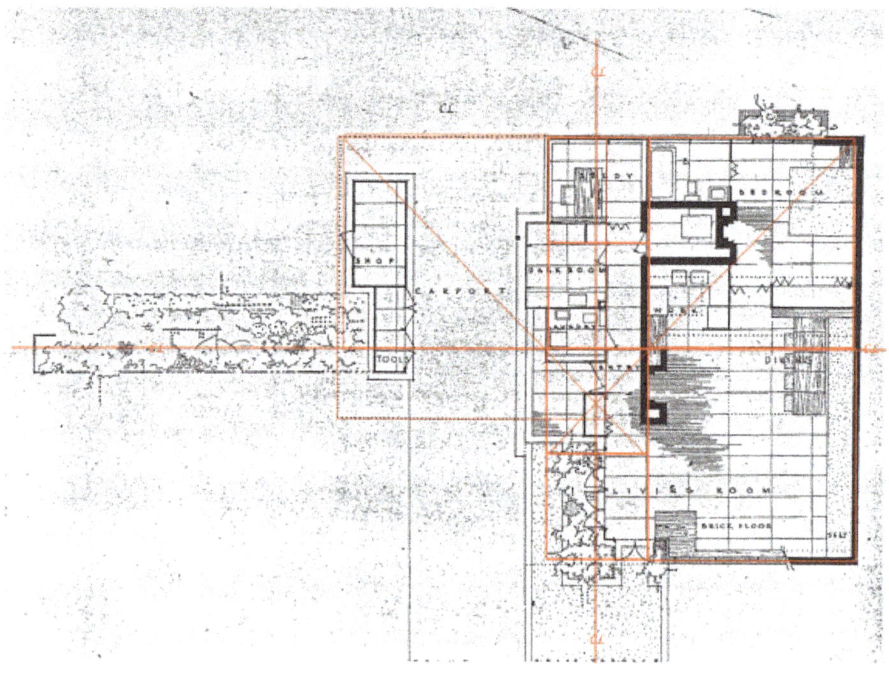

3.1. B.
THE CARPORT ROOF IS BILATERALLY SYMMETRICALLY TO THE LARGE "BEDROOM" SQUARE, MAKING THE LANAI THE CENTERLINE OF THE COMPOSITION.

The carport roof extends leftward from this four-square run for a distance equal to the width of the living spaces, making the run serve as a central axis about which the whole house balances. The whole design, although asymmetrical, is bilaterally symmetrical with respect to its outer dimensions. Both axes are emphasized, by an extended garden horizontally and by a long lanai vertically. These symmetries, although masked by the asymmetry of the elements that define them, help stabilize and give repose to the house as we approach it from the street. (3.1.B.)

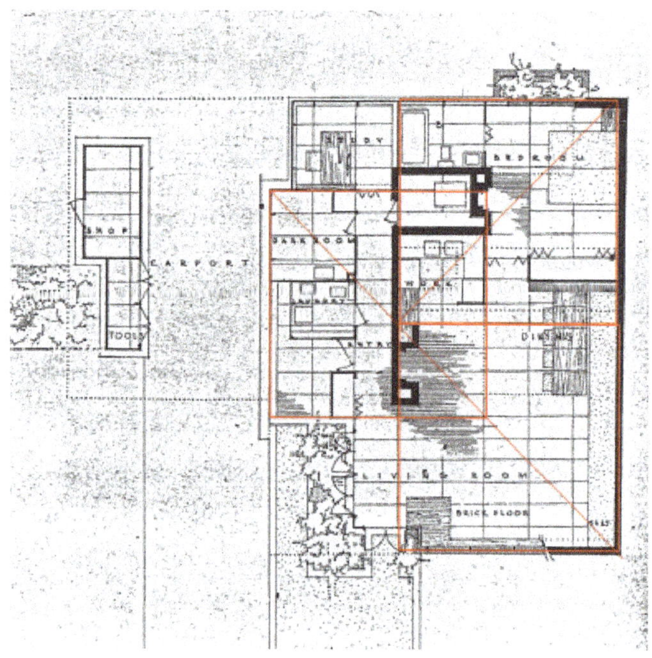

3.1..C.
DEVELOPMENT OF THE ENTRANCE-UTILIITY SIDE OF THE HOUSE: THE LIVING ROOM SQUARE SLIDES UP TO THE LEFT. NOTE THE OVERLAP GENERATES TWO 2-UNIT SQUARES.

As we enter we become aware of irregularities in the outline of the exterior wall. These irregularities are functional and the effect is casual and utilitarian, but their formal genesis is a rigorously disciplined manipulation of the form-making squares. The elements projecting the farthest, the darkroom and the porch, coincide with the left face of a large, 5-unit square whose right face aligns with the fireplace and kitchen wall. This square is the living room square repeated and slid upward and to the left along a shared diagonal. The right edge of the new square and left edges of the original double-square now define the right and left edges of two 2-unit squares with diagonals that coincide with diagonals of the three large 5-unit squares. (3.1.C)

These new 2-unit squares when shifted up one unit and multiplied become part of a quintuple run that defines the bathroom, furnace room, and kitchen and which runs exactly the length of the house. Across the gallery a complementary run of four identical squares circumscribes the darkroom, entry porch, and lanai, generating a local symmetry about the gallery's centerline. (3.1.D.)

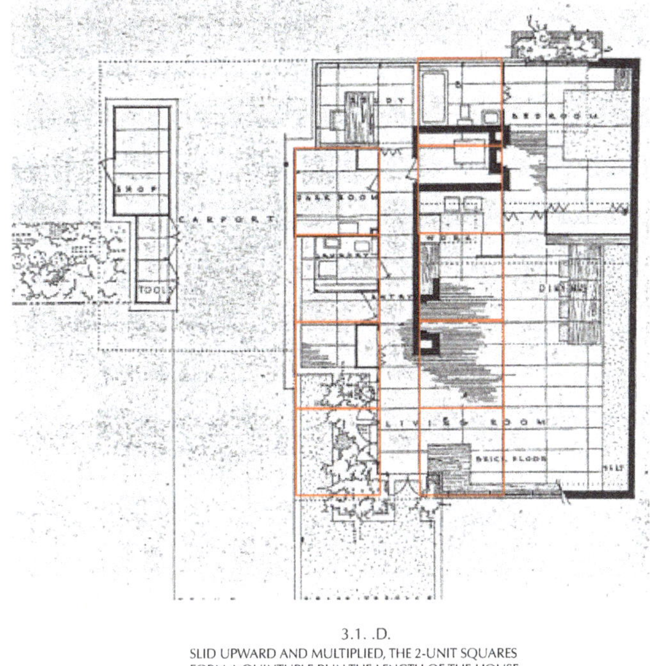

3.1. .D.
SLID UPWARD AND MULTIPLIED, THE 2-UNIT SQUARES FORM A QUINTUPLE RUN THE LENGTH OF THE HOUSE. A FOUR UNIT RUN MIRRORS IT, HELPING DEFINE THE ENTRANCE SIDE.

The four square run just described is overlapped by a run of 1½ unit-squares coincident with the width of the laundry. Six of the squares are generated along a common vertical axis. At the bottom a seventh, slid ½ unit to the right, outlines the lanai planter. (3.1.E.)

Another planter outside the bedroom seems at first glance out of place: why is it there and why is it off the grid? The vertical 2-unit run of five to the left identified earlier provides the clue. If we circumscribe the planter with a square and quintuple it, we find we have generated a similar run of five squares, slightly larger, that neatly terminates at the far exterior wall and along the way coincides with the face of the fireplace on the left and, on the right, with the long continuous built-in seat! (3.1.E.)

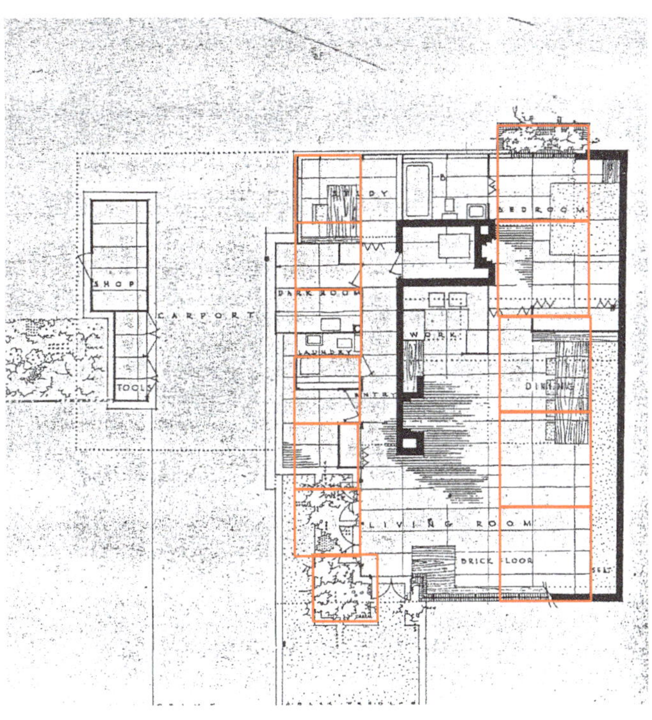

3.1. .E.
SQUARES DO NOT NEED TO CORRESPOND TO GRID DIMENSIONS. A RUN OF FIVE "OFF-THE-GRID" SQUARES INTEGRATE THE BEDROOM PLANTER, RELATING IT TO THE BEDROOM FIREPLACE AND LIVING AREA SEAT.

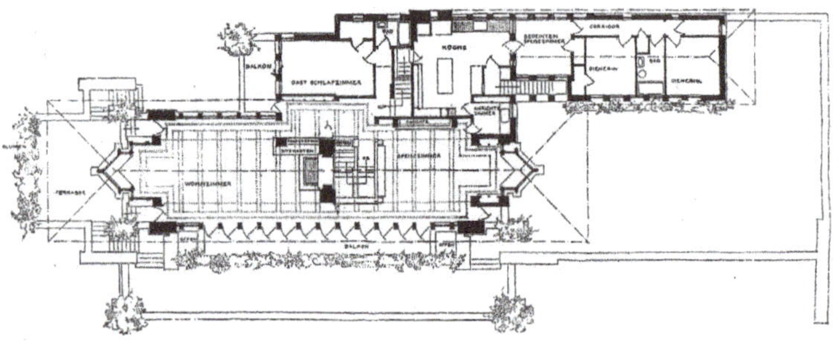

3.2.. THE FREDERICK C. ROBIE HOUSE
1906, CHICAGO, ILLINIOS

The FREDERICK ROBIE HOUSE

Possibly the greatest of the Prairie Houses, the Robie House magnificently combines a powerfully thrusting, energy-charged dynamism with perfect balance and rock-solid rootedness. The boldly cantilevered long roof is beautifully poised over the linear porch and its walled terrace and courtyard. But what law determines that the reach of the cantilevers thrusts far enough to be dramatic but not so far as to appear foolish? The answer lies in the hidden geometry.

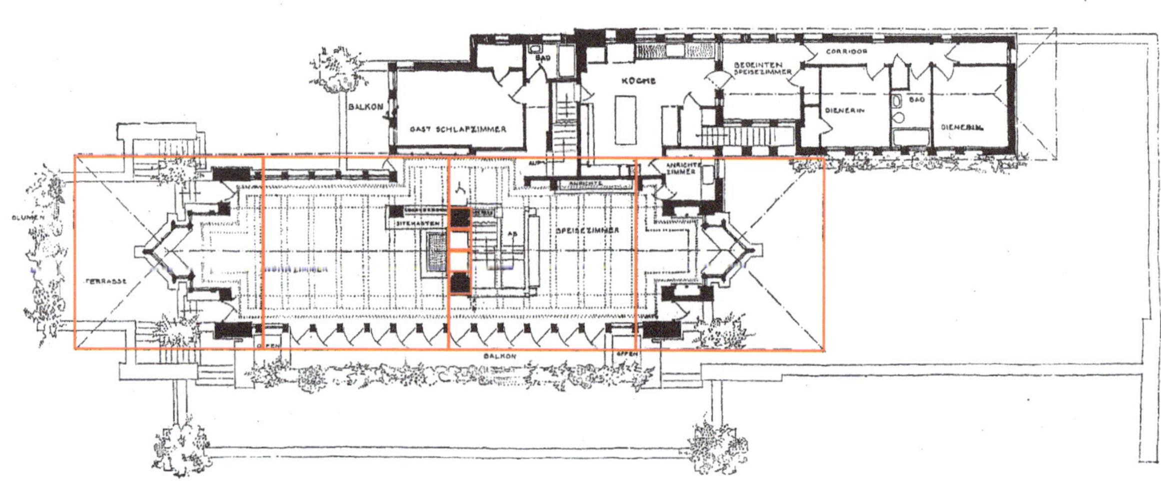

3.2.A. Symmetries begin with the resonant geometries of the central chimney mass and the long roof: both fill the outlines of a double-double-square, or four-square run, but at very different scales.

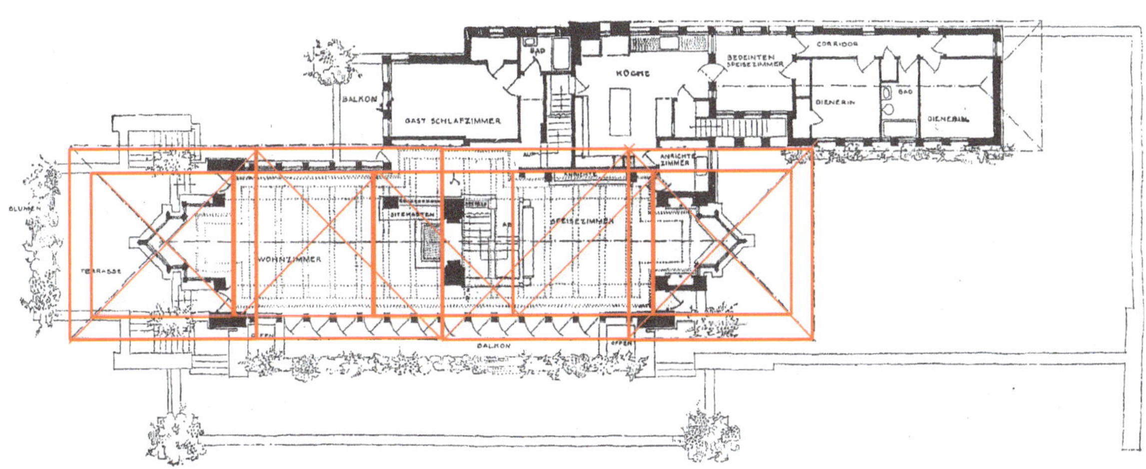

3.2.B. The four-square run outlining the roof grows with concentric symmetry from a spine of five squares that determine the width of the living and dining room.

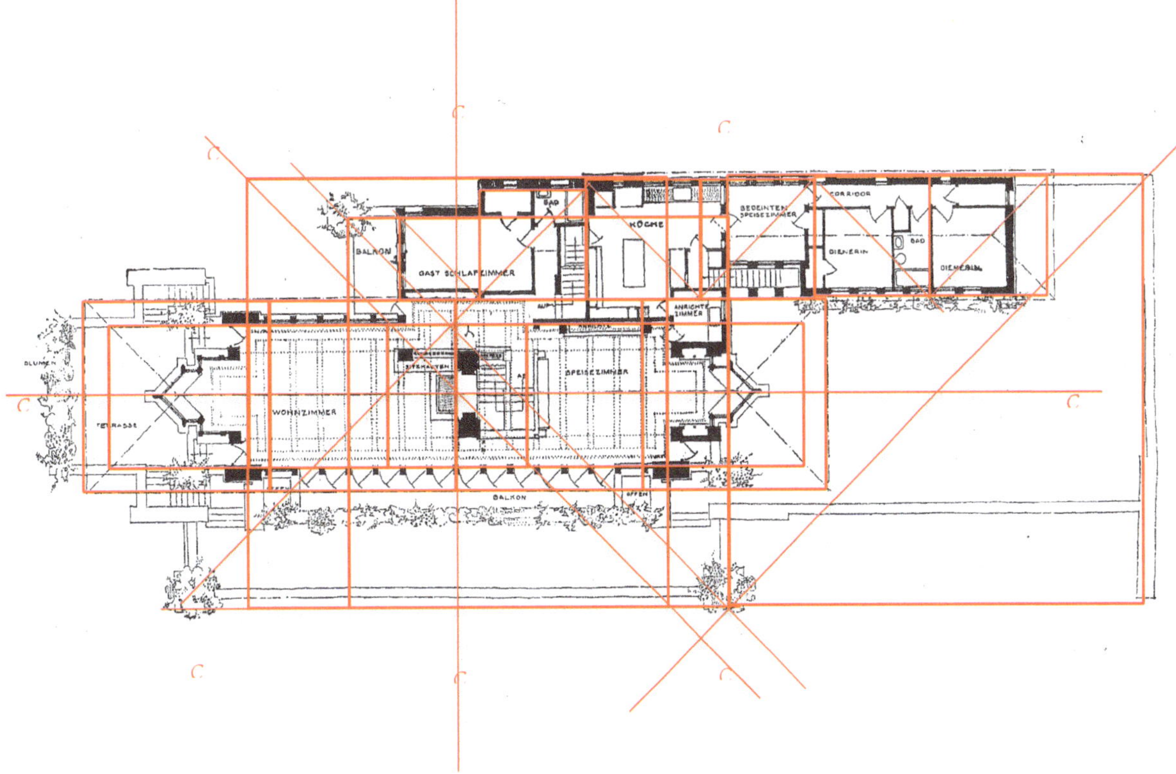

3,2.C. From the inner faces of the two outer squares in the 5-square run is generated a large square whose right and left ends bisect the heavy piers at the outer corners of the living and dining rooms and whose top and bottom faces encompass the rear bedroom wing and the front garden planters, creating a stable foundation about which the main living spaces symmetrically and dramatically unfold. Diagonals extending from the front garden planters lock the rear wing to the rest of the house. One diagonal fixes the rear balcony planter; from the other is generated a square that in turn generates a string of squares outlining the bedroom wing. The right planter touches the left lower corner of a large square that defines the service yard, completing the composition

The GOETSCH-WINKLER HOUSE

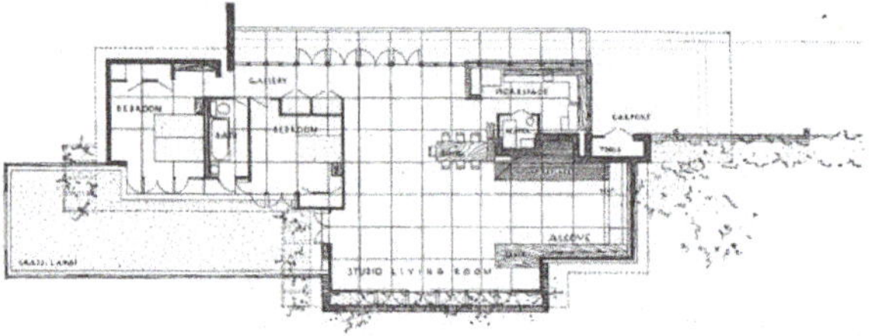

3.3. THE GOETSCH-WINCKLER HOUSE
1939, OKEMOS, MICHIGAN

As his mastery grew, Wright's works became more spare, more economical of form, shedding the conventions of bilaterally placed piers and planters. The Goetsch-Winckler house is considered by the great architectural historian Henry Russell Hitchcock to be "perhaps the best Usonian house in plan".[22] Economically and harmoniously it reduces the living functions to a essential but comfortable minimum.

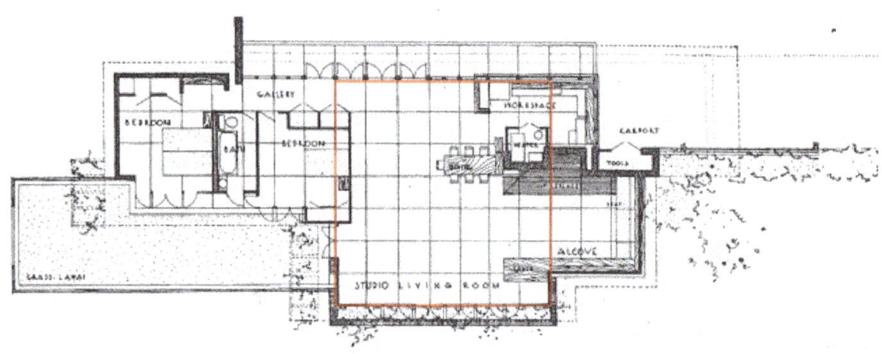

3.3.A. INTRODUCTION OF THE MAIN THEME:
THE SQUARE

Its elegance and simplicity are produced by the clear unfolding of an underlying theme—the square—dramatically introduced by one large 7-unit square that extends from one window wall to the other and runs the width of the living room, centering and stabilizing the living area. (3.3.A.)

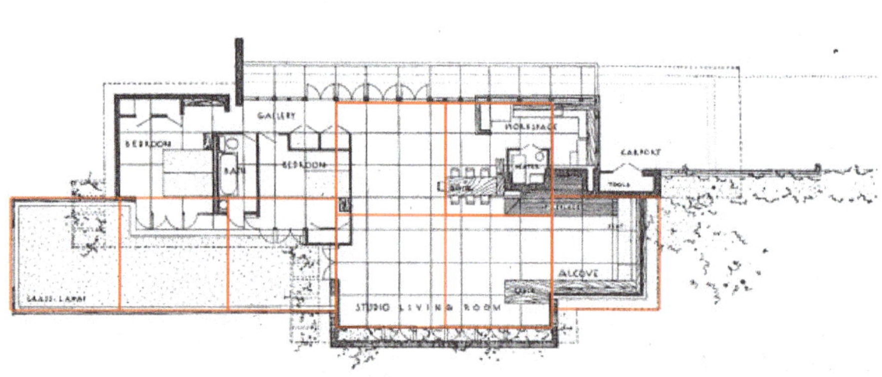

3.3.B. THE SQUARE SUBDIVIDED AND REPEATED
BEGINS TO DEFINE THE HOUSE.

This 7-unit square subdivides into four 3½-unit squares, and these multiply along the lower part of the plan to generate a run of six 3½-unit squares outlining the grass lanai at one end and the outer edges of the alcove roof at the other. (3.3.B.)

Above this run a series of 4-unit squares fixes the carport roof at one end and terminates at the prominent entry pier at the other. A fifth 4-unit square translated down one unit outlines the master bedroom and its porch. (3.3.C.)

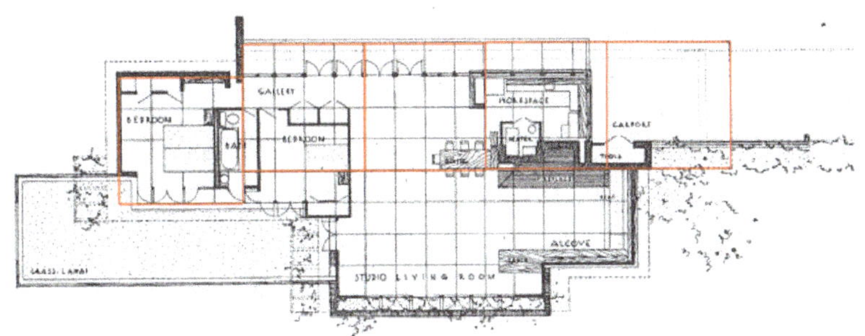

3.3.C. 4-UNIT SQUARES BEGIN TO DEFINE THE ENTRANCE, SERVICE SPACES, AND CARPORT ROOF.

This run, now five squares long, aligns with the roof line but not with the interior walls; but if we slide the run ½ unit to the left, we now find that the vertical sides of two squares coincide with the inner bedroom and the kitchen walls, and the fifth square, when slid downward ½ unit, perfectly coincides with the bedroom rooflines and lower wall. (3.3.D.)

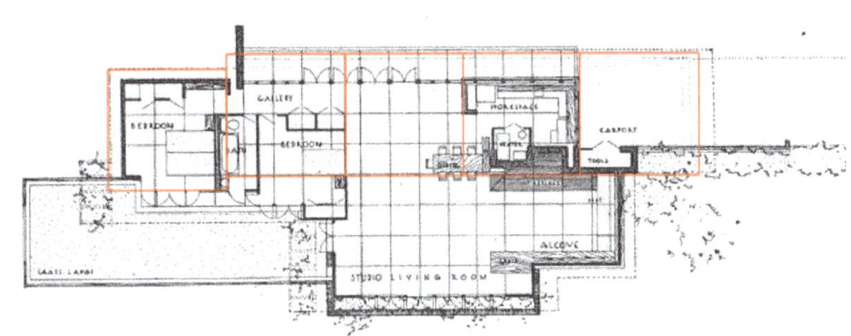

3.3..D. SLID TO LEFT ½ UNIT, THE 4-UNT RUN FURTHER DEFINE THE PLAN.

By the downward extension of diagonals from one of the large 4-unit squares, two 2½-unit squares are generated, forming a double-square one edge of which coincides with the face of the fireplace hearth. Doubling it in turn to the right generates a double-square that encompasses the fireplace/tool shed masonry wall; two squares more generated to the right locate the fascia of the carport roof and the terminus of the extended carport wall. Multiplied to the left, the double-square forms a run that terminates neatly at the master bedroom exterior wall. The lower face of the run coincides with the horizontal centerline of the 7-unit square, and the left end of the dining table marks the vertical centerline of that square, integrating it into the overall composition, and making it a stabilizing counterforce to the incipient rotational motion of the understated but distinct 'pinwheel' configuration of the design. (3.3.E.)

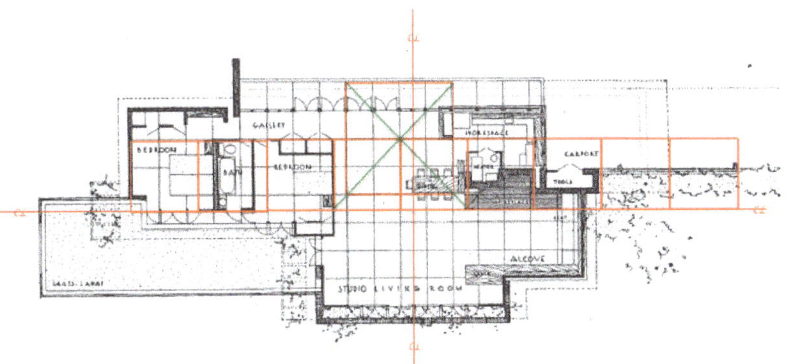

3.3..E. INTERIOR ELEMENTS HINT AT A NARROW HORIZONTAL "BACKBONE". A ROW OF NINE 2½-UNIT SQUARES PROVIDE IT, FIXING SIGNIFICANT DIMENSIONS OF THE PLAN.

The unity of the whole is reinforced by the resonance of form between the long linear spaces and the long linear character of the two primary masonry elements, the prominent pier at the end of the gallery and the fireplace/tool shed wall. Finally, the whole fits neatly into a triad of squares: a double-square envelops the interior to the right of the projecting pier, and outlining the entry and carport roofs; a slightly diminished square projects leftward to the outer edge of the grass lanai. (3.3.F.)

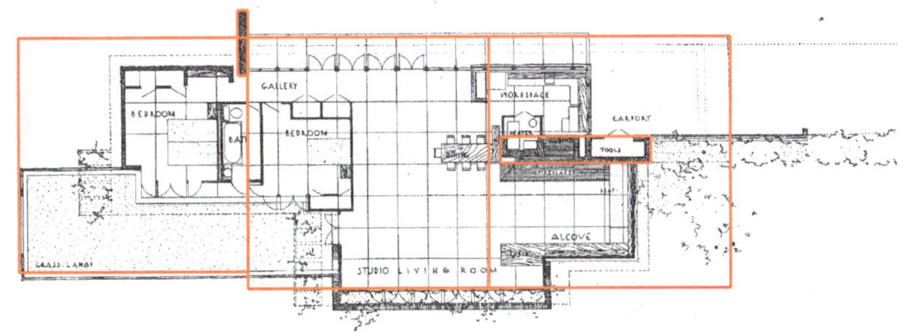

3.3.F. MOST OF THE WHOLE IS CONTAINED IN A TRIAD OF SQUARES.

4

TOOLS and RULES

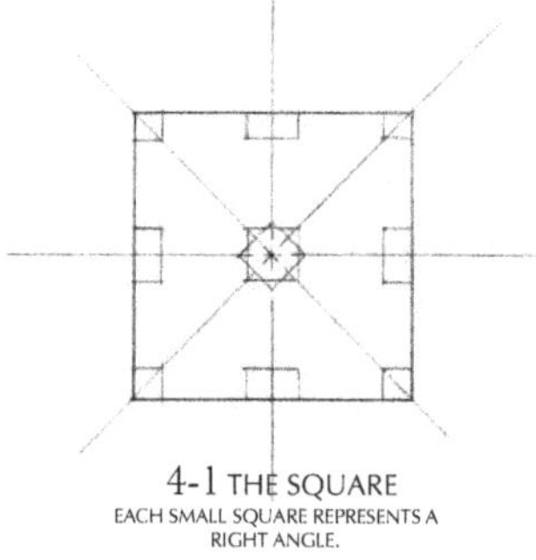

4-1 THE SQUARE
EACH SMALL SQUARE REPRESENTS A RIGHT ANGLE.

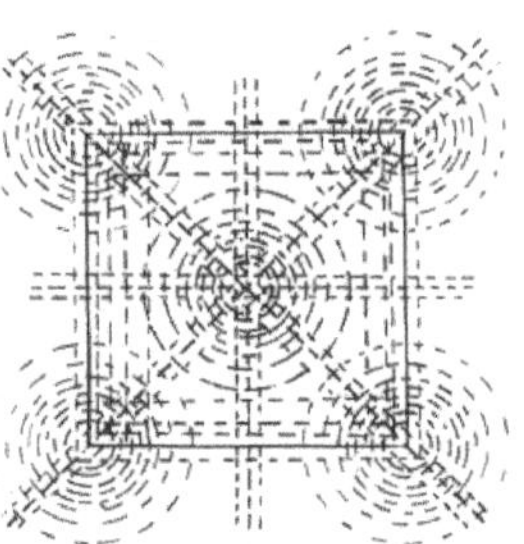

4-2 ARNHEIM'S SQUARE
DOTTED LINES REPRESENT LINES OF FORCE

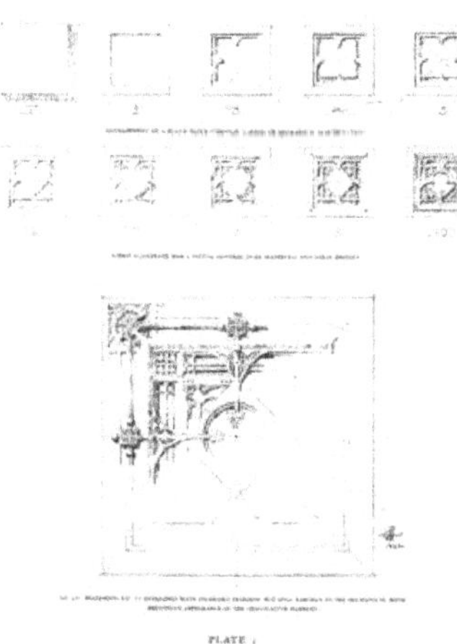

4-3 LOUIS SULLIVAN
DEVELOPMENT OF THE SQUARE

Our three examples are designed on a grid of squares, or double-squares, and are composed of themes generated from the square itself. Later we will see that even in designs dominated by circles, the composition of the circles is disciplined by the symmetries of a square grid. It deserves our close attention.

The square possesses unusually dense symmetry, giving it protean powers of form generation, and it deserves our close attention. It has no fewer than 20 identical right-angled relationships generated by the form and its axes; fourfold-rotational symmetry; and about each of its four axes, bilateral symmetry.

The first scientists to properly understand that perception is a dynamic process, Viennese psychologists of the early 1900s known collectively as the Gestalt school (*gestalt* means wholeness in German), were attracted to the square for its essential simplicity and dense symmetry which, they believed, made it a structure to which the eye and mind were especially responsive. One of them, Rudolf Arnheim, who focused on the psychology of art in particular, asserted that the square has "a complex hidden structure" of lines of force that attract or repel. These he represented graphically. These forces have "a point of attack, a direction, and an intensity...and therefore meet the conditions established by physicists for physical forces."[23] These "lines of force," as his diagram depicts, are the diagonal, vertical, and horizontal axes of the square. The hypothesis that these forces reflected a structure to be found within the brain did not survive modern research, but his insights into the organizing power of the square and its axes have survived.

Louis Sullivan, the great architect who hired and mentored Wright in his youth, identified these same axes as "lines of energy": he wrote that the regular polygons were "containers of radial energy...extensive and intensive...along lines or axes radiating from the center and (or)...along the same lines toward the center."[24] The expressive power of this energy he then demonstrated most poetically and persuasively in a series of drawings that generate organic forms growing outward and inward along the square's diagonal and orthogonal axes.

ΦΦΦ

If a square is quartered by its orthogonal axes, four new squares are produced, and this operation can be repeated *ad infinitum*, increasing or decreasing in size, giving the square a fractal symmetry equaled only by that of the equilateral triangle.

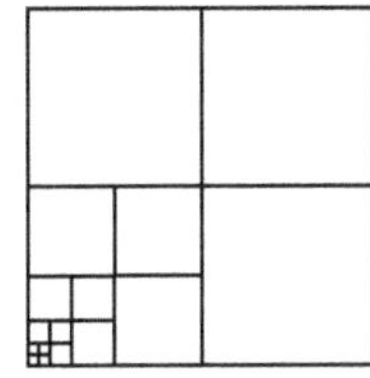

FRACTAL GROWTH OF A SQUARE

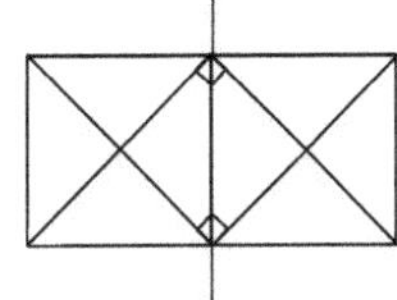

A DOUBLE SQUARE

If the square is doubled, the new double-square gains two right angles at the meeting of the diagonals of the joined squares, strengthening their relationship. The common face of the double-square becomes a vertical axis of symmetry that gives the double-square a privileged place in the repertoire of themes. Wright often generated even highly asymmetrical designs within a double square whose centerline he emphasized by compositional elements, as we saw in the Haynes home and as we will see elsewhere.

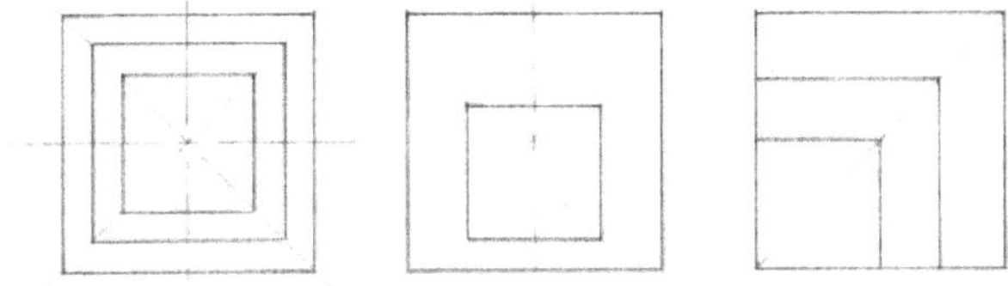

GROWTH ABOUT AN AXIS OR AXES

A square can grow or diminish concentrically, or with bilateral symmetry about one of its axes. Or it can multiply. The expressive power of multiplication is developed with particular effectiveness if the multiplied squares remain identical in size, or if they multiply along an axis of the original. When squares multiply in a row, each contributes its own axes of energy, and the row gathers energy as it grows. Identical squares reproduced contiguously along an orthogonal axis create an especially strong form, for not only are they bound by their common axis but also by the series of right angles formed by the diagonal axes of adjacent squares.

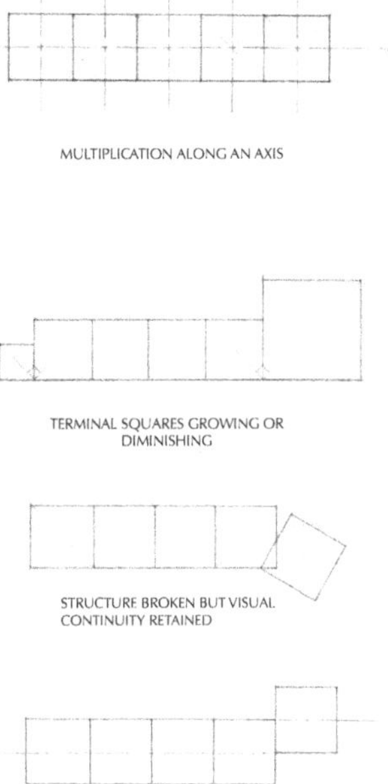

MULTIPLICATION ALONG AN AXIS

TERMINAL SQUARES GROWING OR DIMINISHING

STRUCTURE BROKEN BUT VISUAL CONTINUITY RETAINED

HALF-UNIT VERTICAL TRANSLATION; AXES AND SIDES SWITCH PLACES

Rows of squares can terminate in diminished or expanded units, and the altered units will retain a structural relationship to the run because of the right angle relationship of adjacent diagonals.

Or linear square runs can break the structural relationship but retain an effective visual continuity, if they are of the same size and remain adjacent.

Or the squares can slide ("translate" in mathematical language), as we saw in the Goetsch-Winckler house. Squares that slide by $\frac{1}{2}$ their height are of particular interest because the edge of one aligns with the centerline of the other.

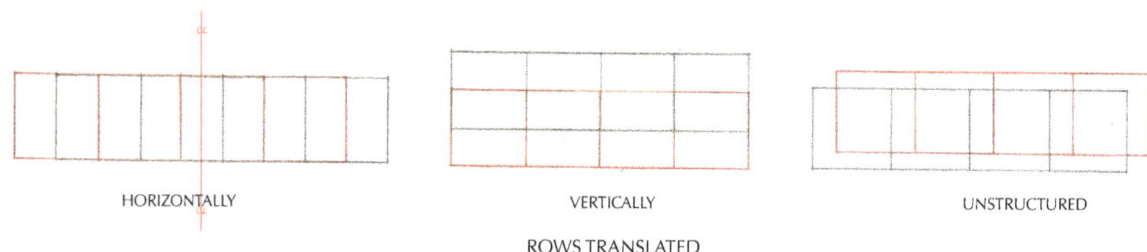

ROWS TRANSLATED

Whole rows can translate along one axis, or along neither.

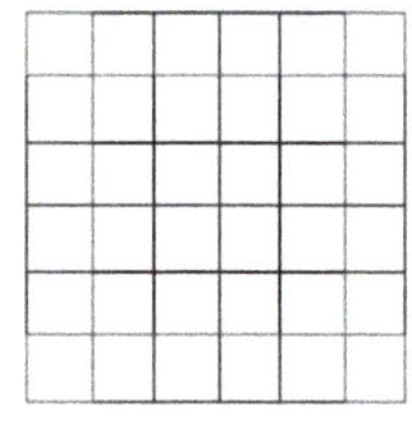

TILING OF A SQUARE

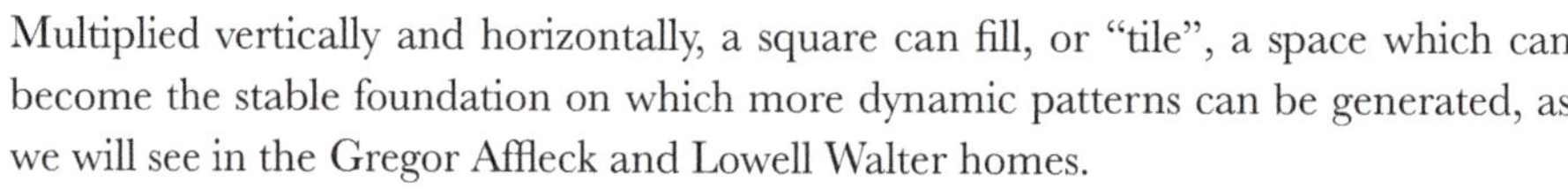

Multiplied vertically and horizontally, a square can fill, or "tile", a space which can become the stable foundation on which more dynamic patterns can be generated, as we will see in the Gregor Affleck and Lowell Walter homes.

ΦΦΦ

Critical to Wright's aesthetic success is the refreshing simplicity of the initial form, of its combinations, and of the ultimate patterns of growth and multiplication.

Common to all is symmetry. In addition to fully exploiting the multiple symmetries of the square (and later, equilateral triangles), Wright used symmetry in at least three ways: First, in the simple use of repetition (symmetry in its mathematical definition is an operation that leaves appearances unchanged; in the case of repetition, the form is repeated but unchanged); Second, in the use of bilateral symmetry, in which two squares joined by a common side are mirror images of each other; Third, by by making a building's termini bilaterally the same in distance from a centerline, even when the building elements are asymmetrical In these cases he often conspicuously marked the centerline, sometimes to the point of making it a prominent feature of the composition, as we saw in the Haynes and Petersen homes. (Why he emphasized these centerlines may be explained by the radically bilaterally symmetrical way in which the eye and mind see the visual field. We will explore this in the next chapter.)

Wright overlapped symmetrical runs that generate asymmetrical patterns but that are often contained within a symmetrical framework. Linear forms creating movement and dynamism were stabilized by large square and double-square forms that frame them, giving firmness and repose to the whole. Plans often grew through the rhythmic alternation of symmetrical form, asymmetrical growth, symmetrical resolution.

It is important to keep in mind that as simple patterns combined to form the final design, each retained its own integrity and therefore its clarity. They combine into a final design only in time, each maintaining its independence as it recycles with the others. It is a dynamic process, requiring duration (even if measured in milliseconds). By adding the fourth dimension of time, our perceptual system clarifies, simplifies, and vivifies the experience of an object that exists in the other three visual dimensions.

ΦΦΦ

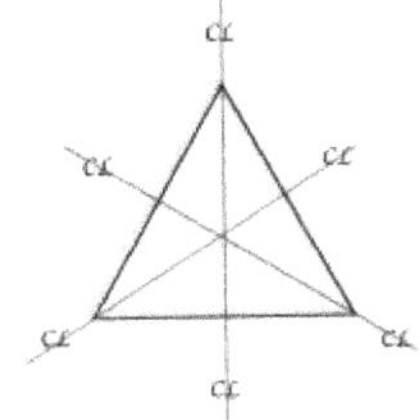

Later in his career, Wright began to experiment with the family of symmetries based on 60° angles—the equilateral triangle, rhombus, and hexagon. These offer a new array of symmetry axes and have unusual fluidity between them. We will notice, however, that even in them the right-angle remains as a prominent compositional element—in the intersections of axes and bases of the triangles, and in the many manifestations of bilateral symmetry.

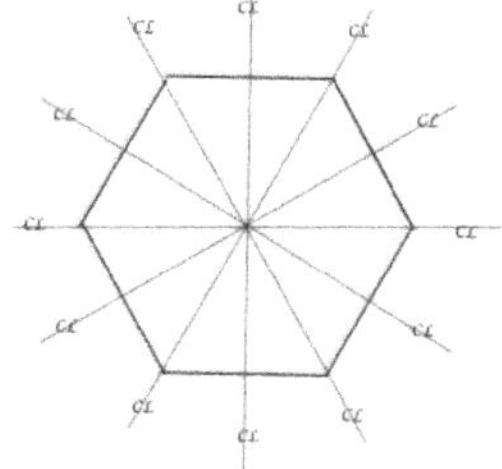

Whether based on triangle, hexagon or square, all his designs unfold in rhythmic alternations of form and inner structure. Often a given combination will be emphasized and repeated, giving a theme and rhythm to the design. Note, for example, the many uses of the doubling of the square, repeated and redoubled and repeated again. In all cases a rich and unique solution grows from the simplest of sources, from "the differentiation of a single, certain simple form…"[25]

ΦΦΦ

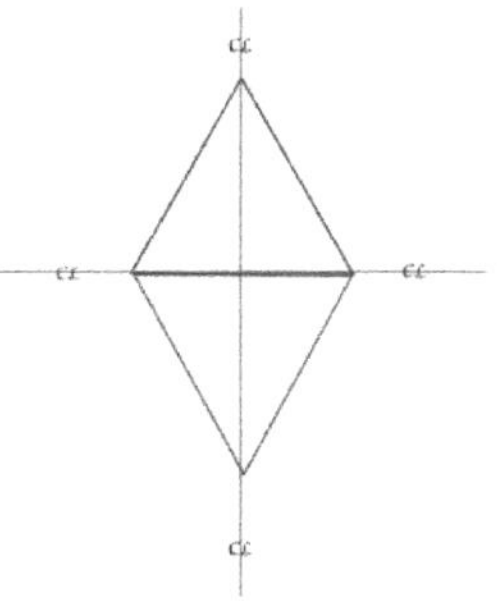

THE HEXAGON-EQUILATERAL TRIANGLE FAMILY

Wright's use of simple forms and his clever exploitation of their symmetries demonstrate an astonishing facility for working within a severe discipline. But is he merely playing a clever game to be enjoyed and analyzed by its cognoscenti? Is this facility enough to explain the deeper feelings his works evoke? If you have come this far in the narrative, it is very likely because you believe it is more than a game. You likely have had encounters with Wright's work that evoked deep feelings, perhaps unexpectedly, and you wonder at their source. The balance, harmony and repose so prevalent in the works, so often in counterpoint to equally palpable vitality and drama, call for a deeper explanation. These experiences surely involve something more intrinsic to our psychological and physical makeup than mere games of geometrical manipulation, no matter how well played.

What explains the sounding of the deeper chords of our being? In the next chapter we will look at the way Wright's plans unfold, I will argue, in accordance with the same symmetries that underlie basic mechanisms and ordering principles of the perceptual process. It is Wright's direct relationship to these symmetries that gave unique vitality, immediacy, and freshness to his works. We will examine the fascinating phenomenon of vision as it bears on the experience of architecture in general, but primarily we will focus on features that bear uniquely on Wright's achievement.

5
TURNING to SCIENCE

Scientists from the fields of psychology, neurobiology, neuroscience, and artificial intelligence have all been drawn to the mysteries of perception; and some have found themselves drawn to perception of a special kind—perception distilled into what we call aesthetic experience. A few have gone so far as to identify a specialized field they call neuroesthetics, wherein they have taken on the question of what makes art expressive. Artists and students of art who join them in this fascinating exploration stand to make some surprising discoveries, not the least of which may be that the foundations of their own calling—creating aesthetic experience—reside in the basic mechanics of our perceptual machinery—so much so that the Arts, heretofore relegated to the status of decorative appendages to "reality" as redefined by Isaac Newton's ascetic laws, may, in fact, hold insights that lead us to further discoveries in the realms of science as well as of art.

SIMPLICITY and ECONOMY: GOALS THAT UNITE ART and SCIENCE

In the field of vision, scientists seek the simplest or most economical visual mechanics that will do the job. They know the mind must solve the enormously complicated task of interpreting retinal inputs in a manner that exceeds neither the mind's memory capacity nor its computing abilities. In addressing the question of what enables us to see in three dimensions, the psychologist Irvin Rock speculates that "the answer may lie in some preference of the mind for solutions that are analogous to the principle of parsimony in science."[26] In addressing the problem of form recognition, the late computational neuroscientist David Marr asked, "...can it be done reasonably inexpensively?"[27]; and psychologist Steven Pinker writes that the problem must be solved "...by some arrangement that minimizes the costs, where cheap equals simple equals probable."[28] In the 1920s the founders of the Gestalt School argued that the mind's preference for simplicity was was *the law* that drove both depth perception and form recognition. Their theories were built on "the principle of parsimony," which asserts, in Arnheim's wording: *Any stimulus pattern tends to be seen in such a way that the resulting structure is as simple as the given conditions permit.* [italics his][29]

According to the gestaltists, this law drives the mind, when given the appropriate cues, to recreate three-dimensional images from two-dimensional retinal data:

> ...the basic principle of depth perception derives from the law of simplicity and indicates that *a pattern will appear three-dimensional when it can be seen as the projection of a three-dimensional situation that is structurally simpler than the two-dimensional one.* [his italics][30]

A favored example was a drawing of the cube, which the eye will spontaneously see as a three-dimensional object rather than as its literal reality as a complex combination of lines on a two-dimensional sheet of paper—because of the inherent simplicity of the cube's geometry. The cube's simplicity lies in the richness of its symmetries: in it all angles and all edges are equal; it is symmetrical many times over. The search for simplicity frequently led the gestaltists to symmetries. More recently, scientists building on their insights, but with a more mathematical approach, have found reinforcement for their findings. Some have analyzed simple figures and broken them down into components that can be coded, and have found that the more the components are identical, the more symmetrical the figure and the more economical the code. For example, of all possible four-sided polygons, the square will be the simplest because its code reduces to two parameters, one for the identical equal-length sides, and one for the right angle.

These scientific explorations have parallels in the accomplishments of talented artists like Wright, who showed extraordinary skill at exploiting simple symmetrical forms. Scientists in the visual fields have conjectured that artists, like scientists, are motivated in their desire to find the simplest laws or forms that underlie their art. The neurobiologist and neuroesthetician) Semir Zeki has written of the visual artists:

> ...the experimentation of artists to reduce the complex of forms into their essentials or, to put it in neurological terms, to try and find out what the essence of form as represented in the brain may be.[31]

Wright himself on the issue of simplicity declared that he sought "the essence of form". In his autobiography he tells how his mentor Louis Sullivan planted the seed:

> "Think in simples" as my old master used to say, - meaning to reduce the whole to its parts in simplest terms, getting back to first principles.[32]

Early in his career, in an article for *The Architectural Record,* he wrote:

> As for the future, the work will grow more truly simple; more expressive with fewer lines; fewer forms; more articulate with less labor; more plastic; more fluent, although more coherent; more organic.[33]

In these words, written when he was 31, Wright committed himself to ever greater simplicity, anticipating that simplicity rather than excess would yield the greater aesthetic satisfaction. It may have been this drive to achieve simplicity, as much as innate talent and early Froebel training, that accounts for the great economy and freshness of his mature work.

From SIMPLICITY to SYMMETRY

The search for simplicity leads inevitably to symmetry. The artists's search and the scientist's converge on symmetry.

For any form capable of symmetry, its *symmetrical* form will be the *simplest* form in which it can be expressed. Symmetries give us the simplest unfolding of any action: pure expressions of an action, unqualified by any asymmetries in its environment.

In Western civilization, the idea of symmetry had its origins as an ideal form of beauty. It was an aesthetic ideal, the goal of the artist. Once symmetry of natural forms were seen by the natural philosophers as shaping the universe—until Newton's three laws replaced them with laws of force and reaction not inherently geometric in character. In our times the arts often dismiss symmetry but in the world of physics, now long removed from Newton's domination, the idea of symmetry in mathematical form is becoming a beacon pointing to new theories. For many physicists, principles of symmetry guide their searches and have led to discoveries that yield not only truth but beauty.[34]

Wright, at least until late in his career, chose the simplest and most densely symmetrical form, the square—of all forms the simplest, most protean, most densely symmetrical. Composed of two orthogonal and two diagonal axes of symmetry each, and tileable, squares can form an endless grid and generate thereon thoroughly integrated, complex, and harmonious compositions. Later he experimented in equilateral triangles and the closely related hexagon. Like the square, they are dense with symmetry: the triangle is composed of three equal sides, three equal 60° angles, and three axes of symmetry; the hexagon has six sides equal, six 120° angles, and six axes of symmetry. 90° angles, found where axes meet the center of a base, continue to play important roles. As we have seen, Wright explored the limits of these forms, but always respecting the discipline they imposed—and making the most of the liberating powers of expression they released.

We should keep these principles of economy, simplicity, and symmetry in mind as we now explore how Frank Lloyd Wright's method may plausibly emerge from basic mechanisms by which the mind organizes perception.

FORM RECOGNITION and FORM CREATION: DAVID MARR and FRANK LLOYD WRIGHT

The brain responds to art by using brain structures involved in perceiving everyday objects.

Anjan Chatterjee p. 13

Frank Lloyd Wright's remarkable achievement is not an isolated summit; it is a quintessential expression of the miracle of vision itself. His method of generating architectural images builds on basic mechanics of perception, and the expressive power of both plans and their three-dimensional realization are in part a function of the directness with which he employs and reveals these mechanics. His method, involving cycling, overlapping, and interweaving patterns that yield forms perpetually dynamic but nonetheless securely interconnected and serenely rooted, flows naturally from the dynamics of the perceptual process.

Wright's method of form *creation* is strongly analogous to a promising theory of form *recognition* developed by the late MIT researcher in artificial intelligence (AI), David Marr.[35] Marr's theory is built on simple geometries and symmetries implicit in forms remarkably similar to those employed by Wright. Wright's method of *generating* forms involves mathematically regular shapes,[36] related and coordinated by their axial relationships, which multiply, grow, and overlap until a complex entity emerges. Similarly, Marr bases his theory of form *recognition* on axial coordinate systems that generate modules that overlap at different scales.

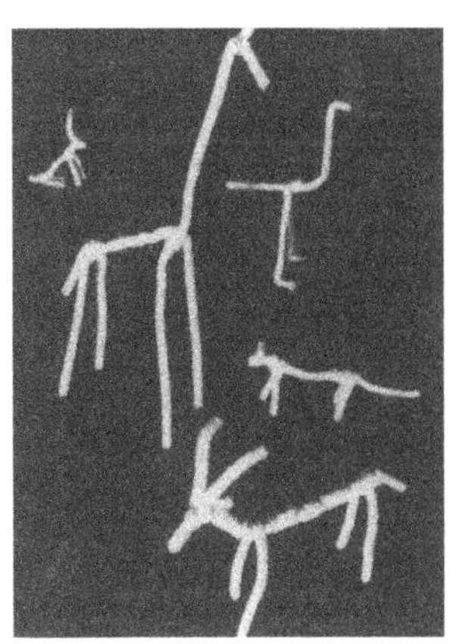

5.1 MARR'S ANIMALS

EACH SECTION OF PIPE CLEANER REPRESENTS THE CENTRAL AXIS OF A PRIMITIVE VOLUME THAT IS A FIRST APPROXIMATION OF THAT BODY SEGMENT.

In Marr's theory individual objects retain a stable identity because are they are defined by dedicated, or "object-centered", coordinate systems that provide a frame of reference about which the detailed characteristics of the object are formed. We recognize the constancy of the frame, and therefore the constancy of the objects for which it is the frame. Marr illustrates this idea rather playfully with pipe cleaner wires bent to form animals.[37] The torso and each limb are each depicted by a piece of wire that represents the long axis along which a moving cross section generates a volume. The axis "may be defined by elongation, symmetry, or even motion (for example, the axis of rotation)".[38] Each volume, or "primitive," gives a first approximation of the body segment it represents.

Turning to the human form, he then postulates that the most efficient and flexible depiction of a form will employ several layers or "modules" of axes at different levels of detail: at the simplest and largest level, one axis will generate an encompassing form that circumscribes the outer reaches of the whole and locates it in space; at the next level, axes generate six primitives that form the head, torso, and our four limbs; from there, more detailed articulations represent the components of each limb and the fingers of each hand.

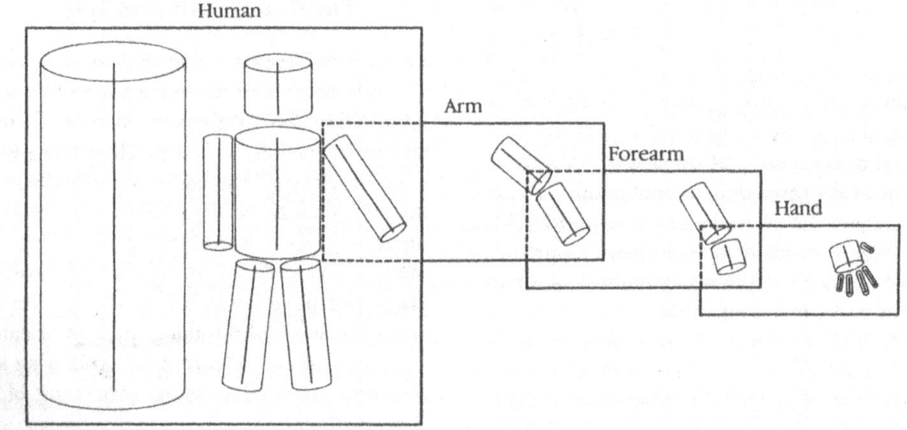

5.2 MARR'S MODULES

Analogously, Wright uses linear forms at different scales that overlap; the largest typically encompasses the whole composition, within which forms composed of smaller units articulate the plan. Forms at different scales are overlapped, usually disciplined in their placement by their common internal structural axes, generating in the end complex but harmonious images. To a considerable extent his method confers the same benefits that Marr derived from a hierarchy of primitives. Marr finds that "The stability of the representation is greatly enhanced by including both large and small primitive descriptions of the shape";[39] similarly, Wright's method of artfully placing more highly articulated patterns within a larger, all-encompassing one enables his plans to command stability, rootedness, and equilibrium while generating considerable internal activity. To confer these benefits, whether in Marr's process or in Wright's, all modules, at every scale, must retain their integrity, even though integrated into a larger, more complex image. They do this by not fusing with other modules in static images, but by remaining independent, cycling and interacting *in time.* The completed image requires time to unfold; it exists only in a duration of time, as a constantly recycling of overlapping patterns. It is an illusion that the visual canvas before us is instantaneously given and everywhere in focus; the mind requires time to generate and stabilize a coherent image from the billions of photons that bombard the retina in ever-changing patterns—ever-changing, because even if both the visual field and the observer remain still, the eye's fovea, the extremely small area where high focus occurs, darts rapidly about the visual field with split-second "saccadic movements," constantly changing what appears on the retinal screen. Color, form, face recognition, motion, and spatial awareness are all processed to some degree independently, in dedicated circuits, sometimes in different intervals of time, before being integrated into a coherent image.

In a very roughly analogous manner, I am suggesting, within the shape-forming circuits of the brain, forms emerge and are perceived only in durations of time.

The dynamic, time-dependent nature of the perceptual process explains rather directly certain seemingly contradictory qualities we experience in Wright's works; a feeling of constant motion, contrasting with a balanced and reposeful ambience; the dynamism of forms that nonetheless remain contained, stable, and rooted. The dynamism is inherent; it follows from the perceptual process; it is the *repose* Wright had to fight for, and which he achieved through his thorough integration and sensitive balancing of forms. This explains why Wright, in seeming contrariety to his flair for architectural drama and the pleasures it clearly gave him, once wrote:

> Repose is the highest quality in the art of architecture, next to integrity, and a reward for integrity.[40]

The psychologist Irving Biederman has suggested that Marr's primitives may pre-exist in our neural wiring in the form of generalized cones, or "geons" (for "geometric ions").[41] Twenty-four in number, they differ from each other according to whether their cross sections are symmetrical, parallel, or expanding or contracting, and according to whether their axes are straight or curved. The geons comprise a vocabulary that the brain stores and draws on to save processing time, selecting them in combinations that can form the first approximation of whatever object it depicts. The discovery of geons, if proved, would come as no surprise to certain important artists; at least two of our greatest in the visual arts have intuitively discovered them, or something very like them, and on them built their art. In a letter to his young friend Emile Bernard, Paul Cézanne advised the painter:

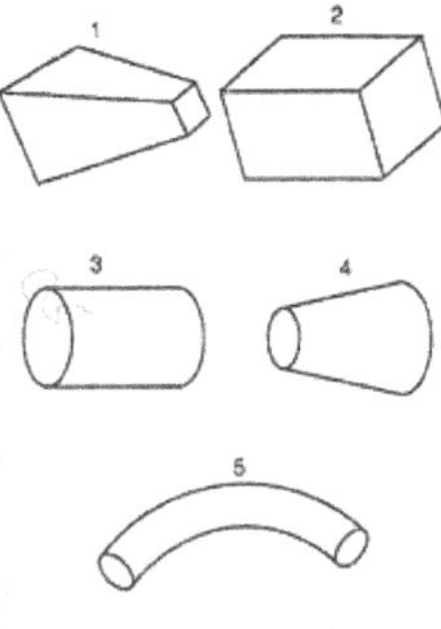

5.3 BIEDERMAN'S GEONS

> Everything in nature is modeled after the sphere, the cone, and the cylinder. If the artist learns to paint according to these simple figures, he will then be able to do all he desires.[42]

In *Towards a New Architecture* Le Corbusier asserted that: "cubes, cones, spheres, cylinders or pyramids are the great primary forms."[43] As for Wright, the squares that he combined in two dimensions to create complex entities in three dimensions could be seen as combinations of geons, squares that rose from the plans to become cubes or cuboids. If Biederman is correct, Wright was making direct use of visual vocabulary hard-wired into our perceptual machinery. This use may be in part responsible for the immediacy and clarity of his works.

Marr has chosen the right circular cylinder[44] as the basic unit, or "primitive," for his modular man, from which he derives two important benefits: First, it affords him a relationship between modular axes that can be calculated, using a cylindrical coordinate system of radii at right angles to the axes to specify the location of one axis relative to another.[45] (5.4). Second, a right circular cylinder has remarkable mathematical properties that enable the accurate translation of its two-dimensional depiction into a three-dimensional image. The plane figures that cap the cylinders are ellipses. As two-dimensional figures, an ellipse is symmetrical, comprised of a minor axis across its shortest distance and a major axis at right angles to it that mark out four identical quadrants; but the ellipse is also mathematically precise as the eccentric depiction of a circle seen in three dimensions, in perspective, its degree of eccentricity determined by the angle from which we view the circle.

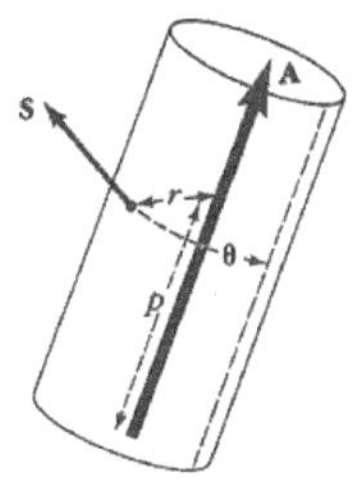

5.4 MARR'S CYLINDRICAL MODULES

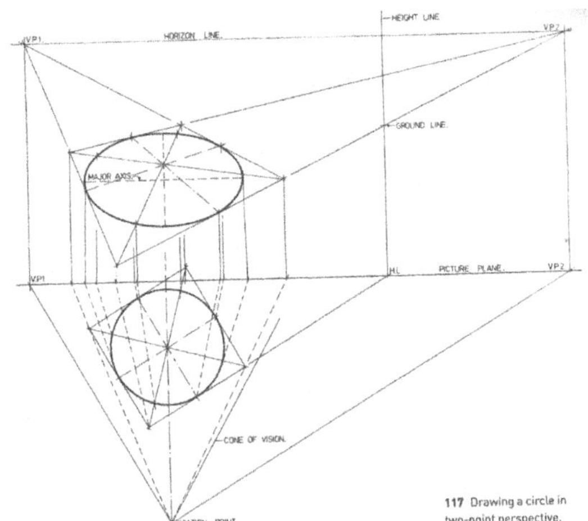

5.5 AN ELLIPSE IS ALSO A CIRCLE SEEN IN PERSPECTIVE.
(NOTE THE AXES OF THE ELLIPSE ARE NOT THE SAME AS DIAMETERS OF THE CIRCLE.)

According to theorists like the gestaltists who argue that the brain seeks the simplest interpretation of visual data, because the circle is simpler than the ellipse the eye will prefer to see an ellipse as a circle in perspective—or in other words, to see a three-dimensional image. (Should the ellipse be generated by a line rotating about a center, varying in length as it generates the form's eccentricity, the eye would be more likely to see the line as rigid, unvarying in length and rotating in three dimensions to produce a circle seen in three dimensions. This is often referred to as *the rigidity heuristic;* we will discuss it further in the section on SPACE.) Furthermore, the minor axis is collinear with the long axis of the cylinder, making the major axis therefore always at right angles to the long axis; the ensemble of ellipses and connecting axes will be seen as a cylinder in perspective, and thus a two-dimensional image is translated into an accurate, more extensive three-dimensional one.

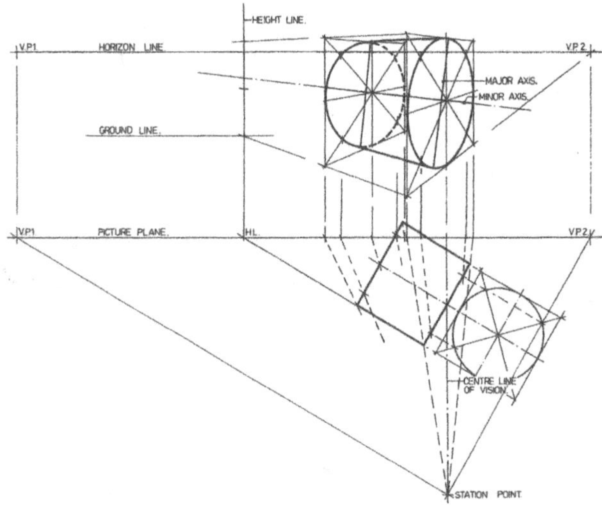

5.6 PERSPECTIVE VIEW OF A CYLINDER
NOTE THE MINOR AND MAJOR AXES OF THE CYLINDER FACE ARE COLLINEAR AND PERPENDICULAR, RESPECTIVELY, TO THE CYLINDER'S LONG INTERIOR AXIS.

The orthogonal coordinate system postulated by Marr that allows the eye to recognize forms are analogous to those employed directly by Louis Sullivan and Frank Lloyd Wright to create forms, and the architects and scientists alike generate their modules or forms symmetrically about them. But with this difference: the axes employed by Wright and Sullivan are energy-laden vectors that generate their designs from the inside out. In the perceptual mechanisms hypothesized by Marr and Biederman, shapes are understood from the outside in, so to speak, and the axes are inferred from the information provided by the surfaces.

To summarize: three essential characteristics shared by Marr's primitives and Wright's primary forms are: their formation about axes; the symmetry of the generalized cones or regular polygons which are formed about the axes; and the overlapping co-existence of these forms, overlapping at different scales, which facilitate articulation of detail while stabilizing the whole.

But for Marr's system, the primitives were only a first step in a process that must become increasingly complicated: the primitives only begin the delineation of the more highly differentiated, often disorderly shapes that comprise our daily experience. For Wright, his "primitives"—the squares with their simple, symmetrical internal structures —sufficed unmodified and he could employ them in pure form. By multiplying and manipulating them in ways that grew from their internal structures, Wright generated from these seminal simple forms endlessly varied and eloquent works of art. These simple forms, residing in the beginnings of the perceptual process, yield the least complex and most economical of perceptual computations. (That is, if we assume that the simpler the computation, the simpler is the neuronal activity required to accomplish it. This seems probable, but it is unproved.) *In his determined search for simplicity, Wright intuitively had gone to the heart of the perceptual process itself, and thereby reaped the reward of great riches from the simplest means—maximum effect from least effort.* As a collateral benefit, he may have shown the world that true art is not mere surface ornament, but a celebration of the very foundations of perception, revealed in their purest form.

ΦΦΦ

Our visual machinery embodies additional skills critical to Wright's discipline: two them—the abilities to count (to three), and to complete an incompletely delineated form—are not difficult to explain. We will deal with them next. A third is one of the great miracles of the perceptual process: the ability of the mind to receive on two-dimensional surfaces (our retinas) all information about our three-dimensional world and to then retranslate that information back into an accurately experienced three-dimensional image. Because of the "inverse optics" problem (that is, any image captured by a two-dimensional surface can have any number of its three-dimensional sources) the mind cannot do this with visual information alone. We will spend some space on this one; the exploration may seem a bit tedious, but it pays large dividends. We will examine how vision must have evolved over eons of time, through the coordination of our visual, kinesthetic, and aural senses. In the end we will we better understand Wright's remarkable ability to conceive in two dimensions and to a remarkable extent present in two-dimensional plans vigorous architectural dramas of three-dimensions. We will also better understand how *all* true architecture clarifies and dramatizes the human experience.

COMPUTATION

Out of Tao, One is born;
Out of One, Two; Out of Two, Three;
Out of Three, the created universe.
Laotse, trans. Lin Yutang

Among the mind's visual processing powers, of particular importance to Wright's method is the mind's ability to count; important because his works usually include runs of squares whose integrity is essential to the aesthetic experience. We must ask: can the eye read the proportions of these runs accurately enough to experience the integrity of their constituent squares? We know the eye responds to the manifold symmetries of a single square, but how correctly does it read the dimensions of multiple squares? There is evidence emerging from current research that the eye apprehends directly small numbers of things (one two, or three) without counting—it "subitizes" them, to use the term used by researchers in the mind's ability to learn language and math.[46] If, as experiments suggest, our minds recognizes two or three adjacent squares, shouldn't it be able to combine this ability with its ability to discern the symmetry of a single square, and therefore recognize directly a one-by-two or one-by-three rectangle? I recently saw this ability demonstrated. A colleague and I had been asked to evaluate a design in which the engineer had been asked to incise a one-by-three running bond on concrete piers. There was enough awkwardness in his work to cause discomfort, but shortly into our examination my colleague asserted: "I don't think these are one-by-three rectangles." We measured; he was correct; the deviation that troubled him was less than 11%!

Once single, double, or triple squares have been established, they can combine to create patterns of greater complexity. Even in his "simplest" plans Wright generates clarity and richness by combining and repeating the simplest forms and combinations.

In some cases, Wright generates a run of squares so long that their two ends cannot be experienced at the same time; yet he carefully retains the integrity of all the squares that comprise it. Can the eye re-assemble temporally disconnected experiences of a run? In such a case does metrical precision matter? A comparison with classical music might help. A piece of music cannot be experienced all at once, but the opening measures set up expectations that are remembered and built upon throughout the piece, and the regular count of the measures provide rhythmic continuity and regular benchmarks that help relate the ending to its origin. The grid in the architect's visual world plays the same role that the measure does in music, and squares or runs of squares form the themes upon whose interactions architectural "music" is composed.

COMPLETION of the FORM

> The sense of vision is not a mechanical recording device. It organizes, completes, and synthesizes the structure found in the particular optical images.
>
> Rudolf Arnheim

THE KANIZSA TRIANGLE

The linear patterns we have uncovered only rarely are completely delineated by architectural elements (walls, etc.); *they must be completed by the eye.* The eye does this spontaneously. The eye's powers in this regard can be seen in a famous optical illusion, the 'Kanizsa triangle', in which the mere outlines of its apexes will cause the eye not only to see a whole triangle, but to see it brighter than and lifted from its surface. In fact, the very incompleteness of some forms in Wright's plans may help create their almost mesmeric hold on the engaged beholder. The neurobiologist Semir Zeki argues that the power of Paul Cézanne's paintings derives in part from unfinished forms and blank sections of canvas that compel the mind to complete the image. Cézanne himself distinguished between *complete* and *unfinished*, explaining that some paintings were *complete* only because forms were left *unfinished*. He wrote his mother:

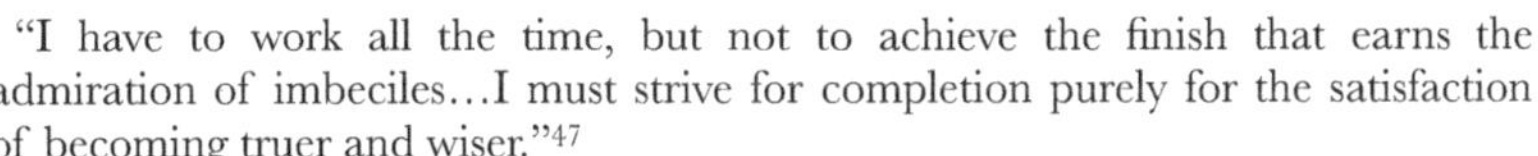

> "I have to work all the time, but not to achieve the finish that earns the admiration of imbeciles...I must strive for completion purely for the satisfaction of becoming truer and wiser."[47]

A friend, the young painter Emile Bernard, recollected Cezanne expressing his belief that the brain and eye played separate roles, the brain organizing what the eye saw:

> Within the painter, [he recollects Cézanne as saying] there are two things: the eye and the brain; they must serve each other. The artist must work at developing them mutually: the eye for the vision of nature and the brain for the logic of organized sensations, which provides the means of expression.[48]

The eye left work for the mind to do, and the mind was thus drawn into the work and made part of it. Cézanne's insight was not new; in the Far East it had been understood and its use mastered many centuries earlier by Taoist landscape painters of the Southern Sung Dynasty. In *The Book of Tea*, Kakuzo Okakura wrote of their works,

> In leaving something unsaid the beholder is given a chance to complete the idea and thus a great masterpiece irresistibly rivets your attention until you seem to become actually a part of it.[49]

In fact, to attain the highest levels of aesthetic experience the beholder *must* participate: "True beauty could be discovered only by one who mentally completed the incomplete."[50] Sometime in the 1920s the Japanese ambassador gave Wright a copy of Okakura's book, which Wright cherished and quoted, years later, as a source of wisdom and confirmation of his own insights. Too late to influence him in his first maturity, the gift was well timed to reinforce his frequent use of the power of the implicit in his designs for the Usonians—from whence they derive much of their extraordinary aesthetic economy.

Cézanne's discoveries and Far Eastern art and philosophy more or less simultaneously entered the volatile intellectual firmament of the late 19th century, a time when ossified frameworks of outworn ideas were breaking down. According to the architectural historian Vincent Scully, that unsettled era was left with but one true belief: "...it believed in continuous movement, in the process of evolutionary change itself."[51] This belief became dominant in Wright's own philosophy. He once exhorted an audience of British architectural students:

> *...the law of organic change is the only thing that mankind can know as beneficial or as actual!* We can only know that all things are in process of flowing in some continuous state of becoming. [The italics, which he rarely used, are his][52]

An odd belief for an architect, who might rather be expected to celebrate the monumental and timeless; but perhaps from this belief came the freedom to express his highly disciplined geometries in a way heretofore deemed impermissible. He might have sensed that his forms had the power, as the Tao masters taught, to "complete the incomplete" in the beholder's eye, and generate an architectural experience that would come, not as one instantaneous and final fusion of forms but as a fluid flow of forms. He might have sensed that he was beginning to create forms that became complete only in time as well as in space, a realization not to be found in the limited science of his day. To move forward as resolutely as he did against that cultural headwind may well have required a truly strong belief in "all things...flowing in some continuous state of becoming."

In any event, what he embraced in philosophy he incorporated in technique. The simple patterns we have identified in his plans do not fuse into one static plan of overlapping images, but retain their independence to generate an aesthetic experience that requires a duration of time to unfold. His simple images—the runs of squares, the squares, the expansions about an axis, etc.—are experienced independently and sequentially by the eye during the brief interval between the retina's receipt of information and the mind's conversion of it into an intelligible image. (For this reason I have not combined the separate patterns in one drawing: it would give the misleading impression that they had simultaneous existence, and in just retribution the resulting image would very likely be congested and unattractive—much like certain regulating line exercises attempted by some of us in our earnest but unfruitful quest for his secrets.)

The time-dependent non-simultaneity of coherent perception may run counter to one's common sense but it is consistent with the nature of perception. The very act of seeing embodies a continuous becoming, as the Chinese artists and, much later, Cézanne understood. Frank Lloyd Wright, committed always to simplicity and economy, brought this discovery to his works, and with it further infused them with freshness and vitality.

From TWO DIMENSIONS To THREE

We must now address a conundrum glaringly evident in Wright's work, much more so than in that of any other architect: that is, so much of the aesthetic power and drama of his *three*-dimensional buildings is determined by a discipline worked out in *two*-dimensional plans.

The first time I presented these analyses to a public audience (at the Chicago Architecture Foundation), someone heatedly complained: "You've shown us a lot about his plans, but nothing at all about the three-dimensional experience of his buildings." I responded, truthfully but inadequately, by paraphrasing Wright's words quoted in Chapter one:

> A good plan is the beginning and the end...its development *in all directions* is inherent-inevitable....Were all elevations of the genuine buildings of the world lost and the ground plans saved, each building would construct itself again. [Italics mine.][53]

I could have quoted as well the brilliant Swiss-French architect Le-Corbusier—probably Wright's only 20th Century's rival for greatness—who was equally emphatic and somewhat more enlightening:

> Mass and surface are the elements by which architecture manifests itself. Mass and surface are determined by the plan. The plan is the generator...The whole structure rises from its base and is developed in accordance with a rule which is written on the ground in the plan...Without plan there can be neither grandeur of aim and expression, nor rhythm, nor mass, nor coherence...The plan bears within itself a primary and pre-determined rhythm: the work is developed in extent and in height following the prescriptions of the plan, with results which can range from the simplest to the most complex, all coming within the same law.[54]

But even the best answer of a master does not fully respond to my auditor, whose complaint, fully understood, raises two questions: First, in the spatially symmetrical three-dimensional universe we inhabit, how do two of its dimensions—those of the plan— so dominate the third? And, second, how does a building conceived in precise proportions when viewed by a designer whose line of sight is at right angles to his drawing, retain its proportions and its aesthetic impact when in final form it is seen in the third-dimension, in perspective, with all the distortions of angles and dimensions inherent in perspective views?

To properly address the second question we must explore the larger question that encompasses it: How can the eye and mind so accurately recreate our three-dimensional world from evidence collected on two-dimensional retinas? We will explore this more fully when we examine the symmetry of space; but we begin by addressing the first question, which asks how can a plan mapped in the planar dimensions control what happens to vertical projections from it.

The answer to that questions is, simply: the ubiquity of Gravity. Gravity severely constrains the freedom of everything that rises from the plan and dictates much of the three-dimensioned building that follows.

GRAVITY

Gravity controls not only the emergence of architectural forms; it shapes our entire spatial existence, with consequences for our experience of architecture. Gravity is our constant companion, precise and implacable; we live and move inescapably within its powerful presence; it controls how we stand and how we move, articulating our experience of the three axes of space, and in particular our experience of all things vertical. As the philosopher Suzanne Langer has written, "Our sense of space is gravitational as much as visual."[55]

In his monumental work *Of Growth and Form,* the great morphologist D'Arcy Wentworth Thompson describes its controlling role with eloquent conciseness:

> Gravitation not only limits the magnitude but controls the form of things. With the help of gravity the quadruped has its back and its belly, and its limbs upon the ground; its sense of fore-and-aft, its head and tail, its bilateral symmetry. *Gravitation influences both our bodies and our minds. We owe to it our sense of the vertical, our knowledge of up-and-down, our conception of the horizontal plane on which we stand, and our discovery of two axes therein, related to the vertical as to one another; it was gravity which taught us to think of three-dimensional space.* [Italics mine.][56]

The constant presence of gravity causes us to seek out or build surfaces perpendicular to its downward force, because on these we can most comfortably resist its pull and on them objects will not inconveniently slide or roll. Relative to them our body, when standing, resolutely seeks to remain perpendicular: it is exquisitely tuned to constantly seek the attitude most efficient at resisting gravity, which it does by means of vision and the inner ear's vestibular system, an orthogonally arranged network of semicircular canals whose moving fluids constantly orient us to gravity's pull. (The eye and inner ear must send corresponding messages; if they don't, we get seasick.)

Our eye sweeps around the vertical axis imposed by gravity, and precisely at right angles to it carves out a line we call the horizon. The horizon is the locus of all the infinite lines of sight in that plane that can emanate from our standpoint. Our feeling of stability within a changing field of vision comes not from having a single, stationary point of view, but from this gravity-imposed horizon. It is gravity that gives us the security of a simple and rigorous frame of reference formed by the triad of: verticality; a plane perpendicular to the vertical in which our line of sight sweeps to the horizon; and a ground plane parallel to the horizon plane but rising (so it appears to us) in the infinite distance to meet it.

The horizon has a dual nature: we reflexively think of it as one with the physical reality we see–the meeting of sky and earth or water (always in the case of large bodies of water; of earth if the terrain is level and the vista vast)–but in fact it is set by our eyes to be at eye level, extended horizontally, perpendicular to the pull of gravity; it is a human artifact. As Emerson correctly wrote (but to make a metaphysical point), "…it is the eye which makes the horizon."[57] The apparent rising of the ground plane to meet the horizon line creates a dual perception of which we rarely take note but which infiltrates our speech: we will talk about going "up the road", or we will say someone is coming "down the road" toward us, even though we know the road to be on a horizontal plane.

WHAT THE RETINA REGISTERS.

By this dual perception, vertical elements that intersect with lines in the ground plane will register on the retina as intersecting the ground plane at irregular, supplementary angles (angles whose sum equals 180°); but because of our innate tendency to project our bodily feelings into those vertical elements, they will be experienced kinesthetically as being perpendicular to a horizontal ground plane.

Essential to gravity's role in educating the visual sense is our innate tendency to project our bodily experience into external forms. Projection is a natural function of the human psyche. As Suzanne Langer, in *Mind: an Essay on Human Feeling*, explains:

> ...the projection of body feeling into symmetrical forms meeting along a straight line is such an elementary act of visual intuition that the forms are actually seen to "balance" the moment the line is upright. Our sense of space is gravitational as much as visual; the similar and opposed figures seem to exert the same pull on the axis so that the apparent tension is resolved only when the axis is erect in our field of vision. *Balance establishes the vertical, and implies the ground line, the horizontal.* [Italics mine][58]

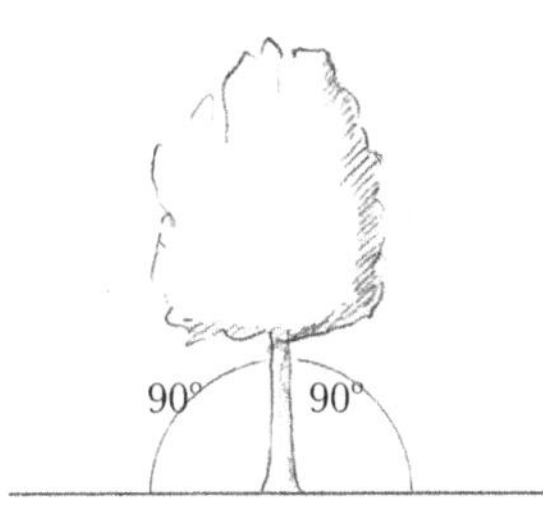

THE REALITY: WHAT OUR KINESTHETIC SENSE TEACHES US TO EXPERIENCE.

In a seminal 20th century work on the character of architectural experience, *The Architecture of Humanism,* Geoffrey Scott emphasizes the role of projection:

> ...this habit of projecting the image of our own functions upon the outside world, of reading the outside world in our own terms....is in fact, the natural way of perceiving and interpreting what we see...[59]

And then applies the insight to architecture:

> *We transcribe architecture into terms of ourselves.* This is the humanism of architecture. The tendency to project the image of our functions into concrete forms is the basis, for architecture, of creative design. [His italics.][60]

Continuing the passage quoted above, Langer gives some sense of the depth and character of projection into vertical elements:

> the symmetrical deployment of figures...expresses our deepest vital feeling, equilibrium, the resting tonus of the whole organism. Its import is simple, but immediately received; the safest device to achieve living form is symmetrical composition.[61]

The need to satisfy this "deepest vital feeling, equilibrium" with "symmetrical composition" of the elements on which we project "the image of our own functions," infuses our experience of what rises vertically from the architect's two-dimensional plan. So there is a trade-off: gravity severely limits what arises from the plan; but what does arise, if well-conceived, gains immeasurably in its emotional import from its dialogue with gravitational force; and in this way the experience of architecture emerges from the very foundations of the perceptual process. Le Corbusier would appear to be literally correct when he wrote, in *Vers Une Architecture (Towards a New Architecture)*:

> Is it not true that great architecture is rooted in the very beginnings of humanity and that it is a direct function of human instinct?[62]

MOTION

Thompson makes reference to our discovery of "*two* axes" within "the horizontal plane on which we stand" which are "related to the vertical as to one another." [i.e.: in each case, related by right angles.] We (and presumably other forward-facing, bilaterally symmetrical animals) experience these two orthogonally related horizontal axes implicitly as we look forward or side to side; and if we move straight ahead we generate and experience them explicitly and precisely. Just as gravitation breaks the spherical symmetry of our surrounding space and generates an axial symmetry, so does motion.: motion creates *motion parallax*, a phenomenon that imposes bilateral symmetry on the space through which we move.

Motion parallax refers to the different rates at which things appear to move past us depending on their distance from us. We are acutely aware of motion parallax when driving through a landscape. Trees along a road we travel move toward us at first slowly, increasing in apparent size, and then whiz past, while a tree line in the distance appears to move with glacial slowness. The degree of apparent change in size and velocity are functions of the changing distance and angle of objects as we move past them: every object on a point in the plane on which we travel moves relative to us at a speed that varies with the distance its image travels on the retina. Points farther away traverse a smaller distance on the retina than those closer, and therefore appear to move more slowly. There is a simple bilateral symmetry generated by this visual activity: as we move forward in a straight line, every point on one side has a bilaterally placed equivalent on the other side. For each such pair, the apparent motion is identical. Points equidistant on either side of our line of motion trace out lines parallel to it, and those at equivalent points on these parallels define a perpendicular cross-axis. Thus motion in a straight line transforms a passive landscape into a lively bilaterally symmetrical orthogonal grid that is experienced as such, despite the perspectival distortion. (The Renaissance artists often made this grid explicit, depicting the ground plane as a pattern of tiles—*pavimento*—that reinforced the illusion of three-dimensions in their compositions.)

If motion is caused not by our movement but by that of an object moving within a stationary field, it generates what visual psychologists call "common fate". Every visible point on the object moves together, and their common movement or "fate," establishes that they belong together. This common fate is one means by which we recognize complex objects; because the various components of an object move as one, they are seen as one; thus the perceiver separates them from their background, and makes sense of the world. Very recently we have seen direct evidence of the critical role of common fate. MIT vision and computational neuroscientist Pawan Sinha and his colleagues gave sight to young Indians born blind, but in pre- or post-adolescence had cataracts removed and lens replaced.[63] The beneficiaries of this surgery at first experienced only a bewildering confusion of colors. It required some time (18 months in the case of one 29-year-old) for the photonic bombardment on the retinas to resolve itself into a world of images that made sense. Objects finally emerged from the confusion, coherent and recognizable, but only after the post-operative patients had spent adequate time in motion, experiencing how objects revealed themselves by the "common fate" of their constituent parts as they clarified their unity and separateness from their surroundings by moving together.

SPACE

Gravity and movement articulate for us the essential structure of three-dimensional space, generating its three orthogonally related axes. But space has a prior, more fundamental symmetry. Space is uniformly homogenous; it emanates outward from any standpoint—including our own—at an equal pace in all directions: it has omni-directional spherical symmetry. As a result, from any given standpoint, in any direction, the dimensions of an object will diminish equally and proportionately as its distance increases, until it disappears into a point on the horizon.

5.7 RAILROAD TRACKS

PARALLEL, BUT RECEDING UNTIL THEY MEET AT THE HORIZON

Just as Gravity provides us a dual perception of perpendiculars, the symmetry of space provides us a dual perception of parallels: any two parallel lines seen from a given standpoint as going to the horizon will diminish in the distance between them in exact proportion to their distance until they appear to meet at the horizon. We see them converging; but we know them to be parallel.

Thus abetted by the symmetries invoked by gravity, by movement, and by space, human beings evolved the ability see the world accurately in three dimensions—despite receiving all visual information on two-dimensional retinas. In fact, man evolved *a strong preference* to translate two-dimensional visual information into three-dimensional images, if given the right cues. The visual psychologist Irvin Rock writes: "We appear to be born with the axiomatic 'assumption' that we are localized within a three-dimensional spatial world."[64] In his experiments, Rock has shown that given the choice, subjects would choose three-dimensional over two-dimensional interpretations of images that allow either interpretation. He had subjects look at oblique lines spreading outward in sequence from a vertical axis. The lines could be interpreted either as remaining in a two-dimensional plane but changing in length and angle or, alternately, as one line rotating in three-dimensional space. Despite the complication of adding the third dimension, his subjects chose to interpret the lines as one line rotating in three-dimensional space.[65]

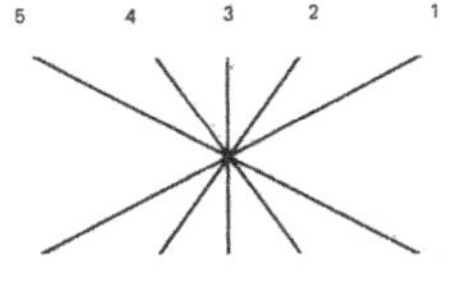

5.8 ROCK'S "ROTATING" LINES.

IN THE EXPERIMENT A LINE WAS SHOWN SEQUENTIALLY IN POSITIONS 1, 2, 3, 4, AND 5, GENERATING THE ILLUSION EITHER OF A LINE CHANGING LENGTH AND ANGLE, OR OF A LINE OF CONSTANT ANGLE ROTATING ABOUT A VERTICAL AXIS OF ROTATION.

In another test, Rock projected a simple figure that alternated with its mirror image about a horizontal centerline.[66] It appeared to be the same figure moving from A to B; but instead of appearing to rotate in the plane in which the figures are presented, it appeared to rotate around a horizontal axis lying in that plane *through three-dimensional space* to its alternate location. This experiment demonstrated not only the eye's facility at rotation, but its preference for a three-dimensional rotation despite the availability of *two* two-dimensional alternatives (those being either a 180° rotation in plan or a change in the shape as it crosses the plane of reflection).

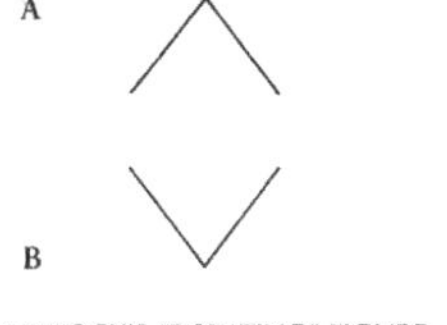

5.9 ROCK'S "ROTATING" FIGURE.

In fact, objects presented in two dimensions that are read as three dimensional can be mentally rotated in a virtual three-dimensional space. "Mental rotation is clearly one of the tricks behind our ability to recognize objects" writes Steven Pinker, who found that subjects in his laboratory will compare two-dimensional figures by mentally rotating them through three-dimensional space until they are superimposed.[67] He and his associate psychologist Michael Tarr and others have presented subjects with drawings of complex figures and similar figures that might or might not be mirror images; when asked to compare them, they found the subjects did so by mentally rotating them.

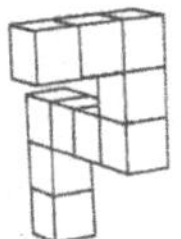

Shown here are two examples of figures that psychologists Roger N. Shepard and Jacqueline Metzler asked their subjects to judge identical or not; they found the subjects did so by mentally rotating one to correspond to the other—and they found that the time required was directly proportional to the degree of rotation required![68]

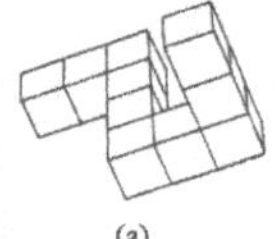

(a)

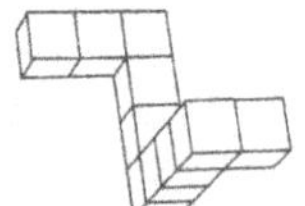

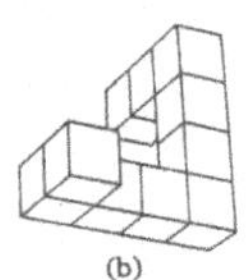

(b)

5.10 SHEPARD AND METZLER'S FIGURES

THE MIND ROTATES THEM IN ORDER TO COMPARE.

The "axiomatic assumption" that we inhabit a three-dimensional world will drive the conversion of a two-dimensional drawing into the perception of a three-dimensional object or space, if the drawing gives appropriate cues. Converging lines by themselves can spontaneously induce a three-dimensional frame of reference within which they are seen as receding parallels. In his book *Art and Visual Perception* Rudolf Arnheim presents a trapezoid that the eye is very quick to read as a bird's eye view of a rectangle lying flat on the ground.[69] The trapezoid has two pairs of opposing sides, each of which, when extended, recedes to a point. The two points fall on a common horizontal that becomes the horizon of a virtual space generated by the eye in which the trapezoid rests. The trapezoid is spontaneously seen as a rectangle, composed of right angles, resting in the ground plane of a three-dimensional space. We are so accustomed to the spontaneity with which we interpret drawings and photographs as three-dimensional objects and scenes that we fail to reflect on how truly remarkable it is: not only do we convert two-dimensional information into a three-dimensional re-imagining of the world, but that we do so automatically and without apparent effort. (Arnheim's trapezoid demonstrates two tendencies of the eye: one, to create a three-dimensional space in which the figure resides, and two, to see four unequal, irregular angles as four right angles and to see the opposite sides not as unequal and angled to each other, but as parallel and equal sides of a rectangle. The eye's strong preference for the symmetry of equal angles and equal, parallel lines is a critical point to which we will return.)

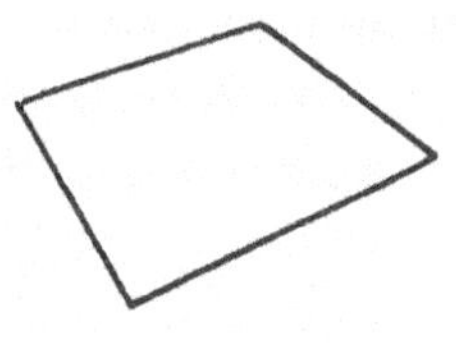

5.11 ARNHEIM'S TRAPEZOID

Our vision has evolved not only to apprehend the three-dimensionality of the world but to do so with absolute correctness. The perceptual process is disciplined by a precise but simple geometry that relates what we see to the standpoint from which we see it. Paradoxically, we best see the power of this geometry when we violate it. The geometry that governs three-dimensional perception, if invoked by a two-dimensional image that triggers a three-dimensional interpretation, controls that interpretation with ruthless efficiency. If the image does not conform it will be distorted by the mind, causing a visual illusion so compelling that we will see what we know to be untrue. For example, Arnheim presents a figure which appears to be a cube in perspective, even though as a perspectival figure it is incorrectly drawn. The parallel sides of the cube should converge; disappointed in its expectation of convergence, the eye compensates: it sees an illusion. Arnheim writes: "the back edges of the cube look somewhat longer than the front edges, so that the top and side faces seem to diverge towards the distance."[70]

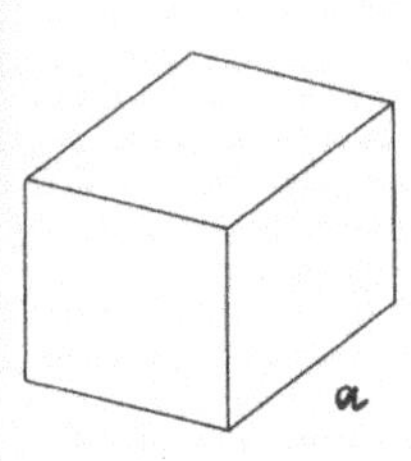

5.12 ARNHEIM'S CUBE

We see an even more dramatic demonstration if we duplicate our photograph of the receding railroad tracks and place them side by side; despite being incontrovertibly identical, the tracks appear to recede at very different angles. The false divergence occurs because a) the eye gets clues that the scene is three-dimensional and b) therefore generates a three-dimensional frame of reference, and finally, c) fits the two photographs into this same frame of reference, according to which parallel pairs of tracks should converge. Because they don't converge (being identical and therefore parallel), according to the eye's logic they must be diverging—and therefore the eye "sees" them as diverging.

5.13 THE SAME PHOTOGRAPH, SIDE BY SIDE!

From TWO DIMENSIONS To THREE: The POWER of PERSPECTIVE

Because of the mind's tendency, when cued, to interpret the eye's two-dimensional input as three-dimensional, and to do so accurately, Wright could accurately see in his mind's eye the three-dimensional outcome of a two-dimensional composition—and with the satisfaction that the quality of carefully chosen proportions would not be lost in the dimensional translation. Thanks to the Renaissance artists who had found the laws of perspective five centuries before him, Wright then had the means to put his vision to paper in a form easily seen and accurately apprehended by the client.

It was the artists and mathematicians of the early Renaissance that first helped us see how things relate in space. Led by the growing humanism of their times, they strove to see and depict the world from man's—not God's—point of view. They were the first to attempt to produce on canvas a "picture" that would replicate what the viewer saw from where the viewer himself stood. They invented a method of pictorial construction that became known as linear perspective, invented and placed before an astonished citizenry of 15th-century Florence by Filippo Brunelleschi, a brilliant engineer and architect, and first presented in writing by Leon Battista Alberti, a polymath, architect, and prolific chronicler of the new Humanism. It has been speculated that Brunelleschi, who was an architect and not a painter, was motivated by a desire not to produce great art but to test scientifically whether the carefully considered proportions of his new architectural order would remain constant and harmonious despite being skewed by the perspective views from which they usually would be seen. In modern terms, Brunelleschi could be said to have been the first to explore the problem of form constancy or invariance under changes of viewpoint. Six hundred years ago he put us on track to better understand all architecture to follow, Wright's in particular.

The artists of Florence felt empowered by a new science that—they thought—taught them how the eye discerned the world and—more broadly—that illuminated the full scope of the emergent inquiries into what would become the natural sciences. But the ardor of that astonishing time cooled, and scientific inquiry in the wake of the Newtonian revolution became based on the non-visible abstractions of his three laws (we will come back to these in the last chapter); perspective and the art it enabled ceased to be the road to Truth and was demoted, if not altogether abandoned, from that high purpose. It was relegated to the artist's toolbox, and as an inessential tool at that.

But the demotion was premature. Linear perspective had clarified two fundamentals critical to our visual machinery, although today we may so unconsciously assume them that we forget their importance: First, the ability to locate precisely the spatial relationship between viewer and the objects viewed; and Second, the concept of the horizon. As post-Darwinians we recognize that linear perspective as a feature of our visual apparatus has evolved because our survival depends on it. In order to survive in our three-dimensional world, we must not only see objects clearly, we must know, precisely, where we stand in relation to them; if the objects are animals, an imperative to flee or pursue may be at stake. With geometric exactitude linear perspective links the position of the viewer to that which is viewed.

But despite the appearance of mathematical precision, as a science measured against modern standards linear perspective is fatally flawed. The range of its geometric correctness is narrow, as even the artists of the Renaissance slowly and imperfectly came to realize. Only at the intersection of the viewer's line of sight and the picture plane perpendicular to it is the object projected with reliable precision; as the eye moves outward away from the central line of sight along the picture plane onto which the observed object is projected, the object becomes increasingly distorted. The distortion occurs partly because as the sight line moves outward from the central line of sight, the distance to the picture plane becomes greater, and objects should become proportionally smaller (as a wide-angle camera will demonstrate). The narrow range of accuracy does not compromise perspective's usefulness as a tool for survival (because the range of visual acuity is also narrow), but in a painting it causes distortion that becomes evident when the sight line from viewer to the picture plane becomes too wide (roughly 25° to 30° from the center line). Piero della Francesca (1415-1492), accomplished equally in painting and mathematics, saw the problem, but like the other artists he thought (as we are likely to do, until we have studied the science) their new discovery recapitulated the eye's own methods. He assumed we see along only one line of sight to a visual field which is everywhere in focus and which can be duplicated on the artist's canvas; as a consequence he assumed that distortion only crops up suddenly at the outer limits of the field. (Even now, instruction manuals give the impression that distortion can be avoided by keeping the drawing within a 45 to 60° viewing angle.)

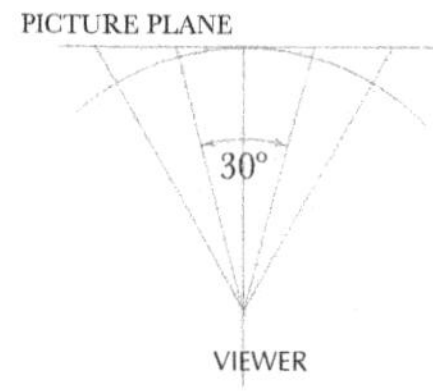

PLAN VIEW

What the Renaissance artists didn't know was something only a modern neuroscientist could tell them: the eye does not focus across the breadth of our field of vision. High resolution is limited to the *fovea*, a dense concentration of narrow-focus neurons at the central 1° of the retina. Surrounding it, spanning 5° of the retina, the *macula lutea* supports high focus in color; beyond that, the retina becomes increasingly unfocused, although increasingly capable of coordinating larger areas of the visual field. Contrary to the belief on which the Renaissance artists based their science, we do not see along a single line of sight a visual field that is instantaneously and everywhere in focus. The physical realities of our visual machinery support a far different model. The fovea flits from one point of interest to another with lightning-quick movements, frequently retracing its steps. The data collected on the retina—from photons of light—is sent by neurons to numerous areas of the brain where different aspects of vision are processed before being brought together in the one grand synthesis that we see. The synthesis gives us not so much a picture as it does a panorama curving around us.

We should note here that the shift from the Renaissance single line of sight to the multiple lines of sight of the rapidly moving fovea appears to reintroduce a problem that Renaissance perspective had solved: their single line of sight provided the geometric fix that located the observer's relationship to the object. The problem seems further accentuated by the manner in which the brain structures perception: it sends visual inputs along two separate pathways, interacting but different in function—the *what* pathway leading to perception of the object, and the *where* pathway that locates the object in the visual field. Nature solves the problem with a single line of sight of her own—she has supplied the brain with so-called gaze-locked, orientation-selective neurons essential to form recognition that will not respond to inputs unless the beholder fixes his gaze in a particular direction. The single line of sight, now combined with others, is reintroduced, locking the *what* to the *where*.[71]

The second fundamental gained from linear perspective—the concept of the horizon—provides the ordering principle that tames and stabilizes the dynamism inherent in current models of perception. The concept of the *horizon*, more than compensates for the loss of the stability that had been provided by the single line of sight and by the uniformly in-focus visual field that the Renaissance artists had postulated and that we were forced by our discoveries to abandon. The concept of the horizon is featured in the very first published depiction of linear perspective, Alberti's *De pittura* of 1435. Alberti presents the drawing of a grid of squares receding into the distance.[72]

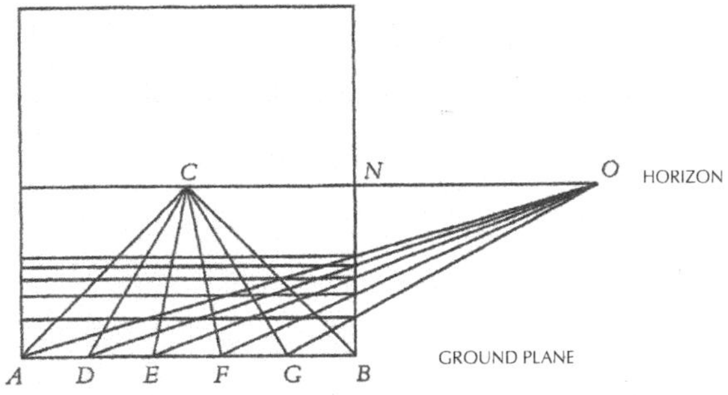

5.14 ALBERTI'S CONSTRUCTION

The drawing is a composite of the side and front views of a grid of tiles on the ground plane as it would be seen by a viewer at "O". This is one point perspective, with all receding lines in parallel with the viewer's line of sight. That line of sight runs from O to the vanishing point "C". This line of sight is horizontal and perpendicular to the vertical plane on which the "picture" is projected. On this picture the viewer sees a scene whose dimensions and proportions are fixed by his standpoint, which determines with geometric exactitude what he sees, and locates him relative to the space created by the picture. The line of sight lies in a plane parallel to the horizontal ground line A to B, and this plane stretches in all directions to the horizon. The horizon is a construct of our vision, constant in its perpendicularity to the implacable vertical pull of gravity. Thus it forms a second plane, parallel to the ground plane that Darcy Thompson identified in his brief lesson on how gravity shapes our experience of the three dimensions.

ΦΦΦ

The structure of the three dimensions within which we live can be stated as a taxonomy of symmetries, beginning with the symmetry of the highest degree, *spherical symmetry*, and progressing through *axial symmetry* to *bilateral symmetry.* By symmetry we mean, in plain but mathematically correct language, manipulations of an object to which it can be subjected with no effect on its appearance: "Change Without Change" as Frank Wilczek, the noble-prize winning physicist, puts it.[73]

Spherical symmetry, the simplest spatial symmetry, is the symmetry of the homogenous space around us. It is this symmetry of our surrounding space which causes, no matter where we stand or in what direction we gaze, parallel lines receding from us to be seen as converging to a distant point, in dimensions proportional to their distance from us.

Gravity gives us *axial symmetry.* Gravity's vertical pull is everywhere at the same right angle to a horizontal ground plane and to a horizontal plane at eye level that extends to the horizon.

As we move in a straight line on the ground plane, by motion parallax we generate *bilateral symmetry,* with its inherent right angles between the line of motion and the equidistant points on either side.

Gravity and motion do not create these symmetries; they *reveal* them to us in ways that stabilize and clarify our experience. These symmetries constitute the geometry of the three-dimensional universe in which we live, three perpendicular directions that translate into a physical system to which we are sentenced (or by which we are freed, depending upon our creativity or our degree of optimism) by our physical, earth-bound, mobile being. These same symmetries are found by artists seeking harmony and clarity and by scientists pursuing laws that govern nature.

SYMMETRY and ARCHITECTURE

Virtually all architectural styles that preceded the modern era were bilaterally symmetrical. Many were created for religious buildings whose primary spaces served stately linear processions that generated motion parallax, virtually recreating the bilateral symmetry of their design—and reinforcing the impressiveness of the occasion. In a sense, the use created the space. But others enclosed homes or public buildings with secular purposes—why the prevalence of bilateral symmetry for them? Bilateral symmetry may be the most immediately apprehensible and comfortable of symmetries, but balanced asymmetrical composition is possible and not too difficult to achieve. Why the longevity and overwhelming popularity of bilateral symmetry?

Let us look at how perception is structured. The eye has its greatest acuity in the fovea, which receives data from within a very narrow space at the center of the retina's visual field, outside of which visual acuity drops off rapidly and symmetrically. Because of the side-by-side placement of the eyes, the field is wider than it is high: this tends to distort the radial symmetry of the drop-off of acuity so that it takes the form of a bilateral symmetry about a vertical axis. Now look at the extraordinary way that eye and mind structure perception of that field. As we look forward, the *left* half of our field of vision is registered only by the *right* side of the retina of *both* eyes, and correspondingly the *right* half of the field is registered only by the *left* sides of the two retinas; the signals are then conveyed along separate neural pathways until they are finally coordinated in the visual cortex at the back of the brain. Why would the pathways to perception evolve in such a way? Perhaps it is because our vision evolved not only to give us an accurate representation of the world but, equally importantly, to give us our precise location and direction within that world. This is ensured by dividing left and right so radically. (The failure of one these pathways causes a bizarre disability. Called hemispherical neglect, its victims see only one-half of what is in front of them, and do not know the other half is missing. It is an extremely disorienting condition.)

Bilateral symmetry may also be favored because as the eye learns a new object, it has a propensity to learn the object's mirror image as well. Researchers trying to understand dyslexia, whose chief symptom is difficulty in distinguishing letters that can be paired as mirror images (such as 'p' and 'q', and 'b' and 'd') have theorized that it is caused in part by this mirror imaging, a propensity so fundamental to the learning process that even the normal child first learning to read transposes letters and words, and can often read and write backward, as if a precocious Leonardo da Vinci! Normal students lose this ability as the brain teaches them to see their letters "properly"—that is, in only one orientation. This seemingly indirect path to reading competence occurs, these scientists believe, because in order to develop a written language man has adapted visual mechanisms that had evolved for quite another purpose. It haas been suggested that the brain automatically processes images so we see the object and its mirror image to simplify the recognition of objects in our environment—including threatening ones, like tigers—that look the same whether attacking us from the left or the right. Symmetrical views about the horizontal or longitudinal axes do not confer the same advantages! [74]

Although his later buildings became most emphatically asymmetrical, and long after he had banished overt expressions of bilateral symmetry, Wright nonetheless continued to place asymmetrical plans within hidden bilaterally symmetrical frameworks, often with the centerlines (usually the vertical ones) of those frames emphasized.

This central focus concentrates both the efforts of the creator and the attention of the beholder. Try this experiment with one of the plans for which the vertical centerline has been identified: focus on the centerline, but take in the whole composition, paying particular attention to the masonry elements. The arrangement of these elements, which may have seemed pleasing and correct before, will now have a special liveliness. The elements create intervals between them that breathe and an overall pattern that is alive but also balanced and stable, even serene.[75]

By responding forthrightly to the eye's form-recognizing and orientation-fixing mechanisms, the great architects intuitively produced the forms that had the greatest power to please not only the kinesthetic sympathies of the body but the convenience of the eye. Wright, by continuing the use of symmetrical frameworks underlying carefully balanced asymmetrical compositions, retained the strengths of the former while generating great richness from the latter.

A LIMITED THEORY of AESTHETICS

Wright's discipline originates in the economical employment of mechanisms of perception found in early stages of the perceptual process, mechanisms which in turn are built on economies inherent in elemental symmetries. Is the "severe discipline" with which Wright employed economy of forms and of formal manipulations, facilitated by economical visual mechanics, as responsible as he asserted it is for the "vitality and magic" that flow from his plans and buildings? To explore this question we must enter into the thickets of aesthetic theory.

What I propose is a theory limited to that aesthetic experience which is spontaneously engendered; that is, which is responsive to forms uncolored by previous experience or training. We acknowledge that the totality of aesthetic experience includes more than this—includes, inherently and inevitably, resonances of associations from our past; of emotional responses to the subject matter; and, possibly, of intimations of underlying archetypes. Architecture, being non-figurative, does not present human subjects to whom we might empathetically or emotionally engage, but it is literally home for some our most strongly felt needs—safe and comfortable shelter for homes or communal spaces, and spiritual needs provided for by religious edifices or holy spaces.

True architecture provides for these needs physically but in addition responds to the depths of emotion that these needs call forth. For example, the heavy, simple mass of the sweeping, dramatically cantilevered roof of the Robie house, in addition to providing protection from the rain, engenders a strong sense of shelter: this home is *experienced* above all as a sheltering edifice. The feeling of shelter the roof conveys cannot be separated from the purely aesthetic contribution it makes to a magnificent piece of sculpture. In weighty mass and bold outline it rests perfectly poised above the masonry masses beneath that give it literal and virtual support; and its dynamic, thrusting quality is in perfectly balanced counterpoint to the ground-securing, pyramidal massing of the whole.

With due recognition to their inherent relatedness to other sources of emotion, our theory purports to explain only those aesthetic qualities given immediately to the senses; qualities that follow from the machinery of perception at work as it makes intelligible what registers on the retina, all occurring in the milliseconds of time before conscious apprehension of the image.

This theory of beauty is not new, although, as we state it here, modern discoveries of the visual process and of Wright's "hidden" geometries give contemporary amplification to it. "Unity in variety" is the theory's popular formulation. In concise form it asserts that beauty depends not only on the final richness and complexity of its object, but also on the simplicity of the formal sources from which the richness and complexity emerge. It argues that aesthetic rewards follow from the achievement of maximum effects from minimal means.

The eminent 20th-century mathematician George Birkhoff (1884-1944) presented the theory in the ascetic language of mathematics. After taking care to differentiate between aesthetic feeling due to the sensory experience of an object, to which his theory applies, and aesthetic feeling engendered by connotations that attach to the formed object, to which it does not, he presented the theory this way:

> *Aesthetic measure (M)* equals the art object's "harmony, symmetry, or *order (O)*," divided by *Complexity (C)* [Italics his]. M = O/C.

Because "Order," which he referred to as "the density of order relations in the aesthetic object" is the numerator, and "complexity" the denominator, the less the complexity and the more numerous the order relationships, the greater is the aesthetic satisfaction.[76] This is not reductionism gone mad; it is one form of a maxim widely embraced by artists and followed, perhaps intuitively, in creating their art: Maximum effect from minimum means produces aesthetic quality. Some artists were aware that they lived by such a law; recall that Le Corbusier and Cézanne invoked the simplest solids as the building blocks of their works, and Louis Sullivan's admonishment to Wright that he should "think in simples." Wright himself fleshed out Birkhoff's formula by example when he declared Beethoven's 5th symphony:

> ...the noblest thought-built edifice in our world...a tumult and splendor of sound built on four repeated tones based upon a rhythm a child could play on the piano with one finger.[77]

Of course he was describing the aural equivalent of his own great achievements, wherein dense and harmonious fabrics of design were woven from the dense symmetries of the simple square or equilateral triangle.

One can press the question further and ask, Even granting demonstrable virtuosity or the seemingly magical generation of complex harmonies from simple sources, doesn't great art hint at deeper aesthetic meanings? The physicist Frank Wilczek believes that *in his field* the discovery of simple patterns that underlie apparent complexity give pleasure because they are a form of learning, and, he goes on to argue, we are programmed to learn:

> ...by interacting with the world, forming expectations, and comparing our predictions with reality. When we form expectations that turn out to be correct, we experience pleasure and satisfaction. Those reward mechanisms encourage successful learning. They also stimulate—indeed, at base they are *are*—our sense of beauty. [Italics his.][78]

He then argues that two attributes, *symmetry* and *economy*, whose importance to art and science have been a constant theme of this essay, are lodestones for discovery and therefore sources of beauty.

> ...Nature employs, in her basic workings, symmetry and economy of means. For these principles...promote successful prediction and learning. From the appearance of part of a symmetric object we can predict (successfully!) the appearance of the rest;... Symmetry and economy of means, therefore, are exactly the sorts of things we are apt to experience as beautiful.[79]

For Wilczek, beauty and truth come together, and his meditations lead to connections between natural laws and the foundations of art. His argument that the experience of beauty is the reward for learning may suggest the inference that beauty serves only a pragmatic function, but both scientist and artist might argue with that; in their aspirations they appear to be reaching for something higher and, sometimes, converge on discoveries where beauty and truth come together (albeit in form more austere and abstract for the scientist, more visible and sensuous for the visual artist), giving intimations of a universe that embodies both.

6

MORE CASE STUDIES

These examples were all taken from choices made first by Wright himself, for publication in his books, in two *Architectural Forums* (January 1938 and January 1948), or in books produced with co-editors. The analyses you see were all done on the plans as he presented them in these formats (and thus the slight variations in presentation style the reader will encounter.)

From among them I chose examples that would suggest the extraordinary variety of themes and styles that could emerge from the masterful exercise of his discipline. The more analyses I undertook, the more I found myself marveling at a series of unique twists on what I thought had become a familiar technique. I came to believe that Wright deliberately put himself on a voyage of discovery, probably treating each new commission as a opportunity to explore the seemingly infinite expressive range of forms and effects his discipline could generate.

Throughout them all we find harmony and balance; but look as well for unusually clever developments of themes and for unusually thorough integrations of the whole. Above all, observe that throughout the unique features in each were never arbitrarily chosen for effect, but were the inevitable result of growth coordinated from the inside out.

The THOMAS E. KEYS HOUSE

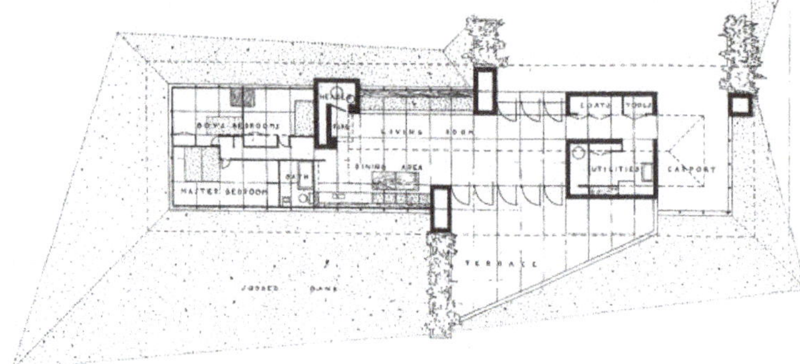

6.1 THOMAS E. KEYS HOUSE
1951, ROCHESTER, MINNESOTA

Built in 1951, it was limited by budget to plain materials and a minimum of formal complication. Wright called it a 'berm type", which he considered practical and economical.

It is a linear plan, seemingly casual in layout. But despite the casual appearance, the plan is generated by the highly disciplined integration of nested runs of squares.

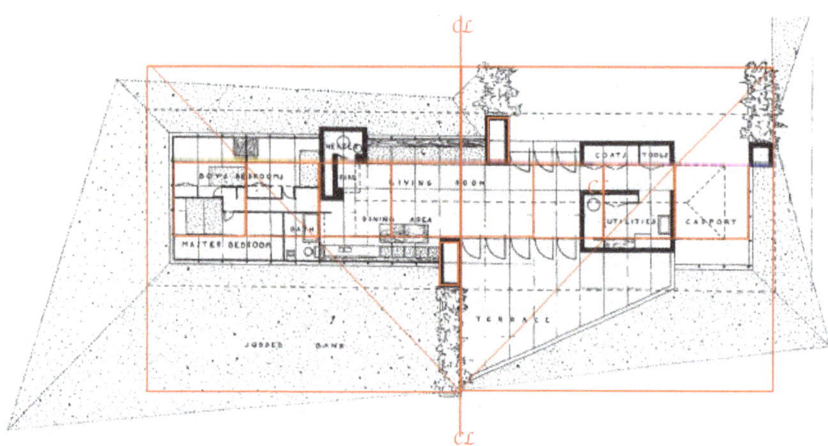

6.1 A. OPENING THEME: DOUBLE SQUARES

The integration begins with the geometric similarity of the central masonry piers and the plan's all-encompassing envelope: in plan, both piers and envelope are double-squares. An all encompassing double-square is defined at top and bottom by the outer faces of the planters and at its left and right ends by the roof edges. Its vertical centerline coincides with the face of the longest vertical element in the plan, the long planter that borders the left end of the terrace. Along two diagonals of these encompassing squares are generated smaller, 3-unit squares, which, if multiplied along their horizontal axis, give us the edges of the hip and the outermost walls of the house and its carport. This places the house symmetrically within the encompassing double square, and gives us a strong axial spine about which the plan unfolds. (6.1.A.)

Two of the 3-unit squares grow concentrically to yield 5-unit squares that establish the exterior walls and, when multiplied to give us a run of five 5-unit squares, fix the exterior wall at the left end and the outer edge of the roof at the right end. The outer carport pier is there to receive this run and to mediate between the 5-unit series and the 3-unit spine. Note that both the 3-unit and 5-unit runs cannot coincide at both ends, inasmuch as eight 3-unit squares span 24 units, and five 5-unit squares span 25. But Wright turns this to advantage: by making the larger squares correspond with the exterior wall at one end and the roof edge at the other, he ties roof and wall together. (6.1.B)

If this run is then shifted laterally to the left by one unit, the roof and wall correspondences switch places, and this combined pair of operations generates a sequential bilateral symmetry whose center is the halfway point between the outer edges of the roof. (We will use the term 'dynamic symmetry' to denote symmetries formed by such paired operations.) (6.1.C)

Returning now to the run of 5-unit squares: if we take the middle three squares and shift them up ½ unit and to the right one unit, we find this new series exactly circumscribes the outer faces of the two major masonry elements. (6.1.D.)

Finally, we expand our squares outward to the upper and lower rooflines, generating 7-unit squares, of which a series of three exactly contain the outer reaches of the main body of the house. (6.1.E .)

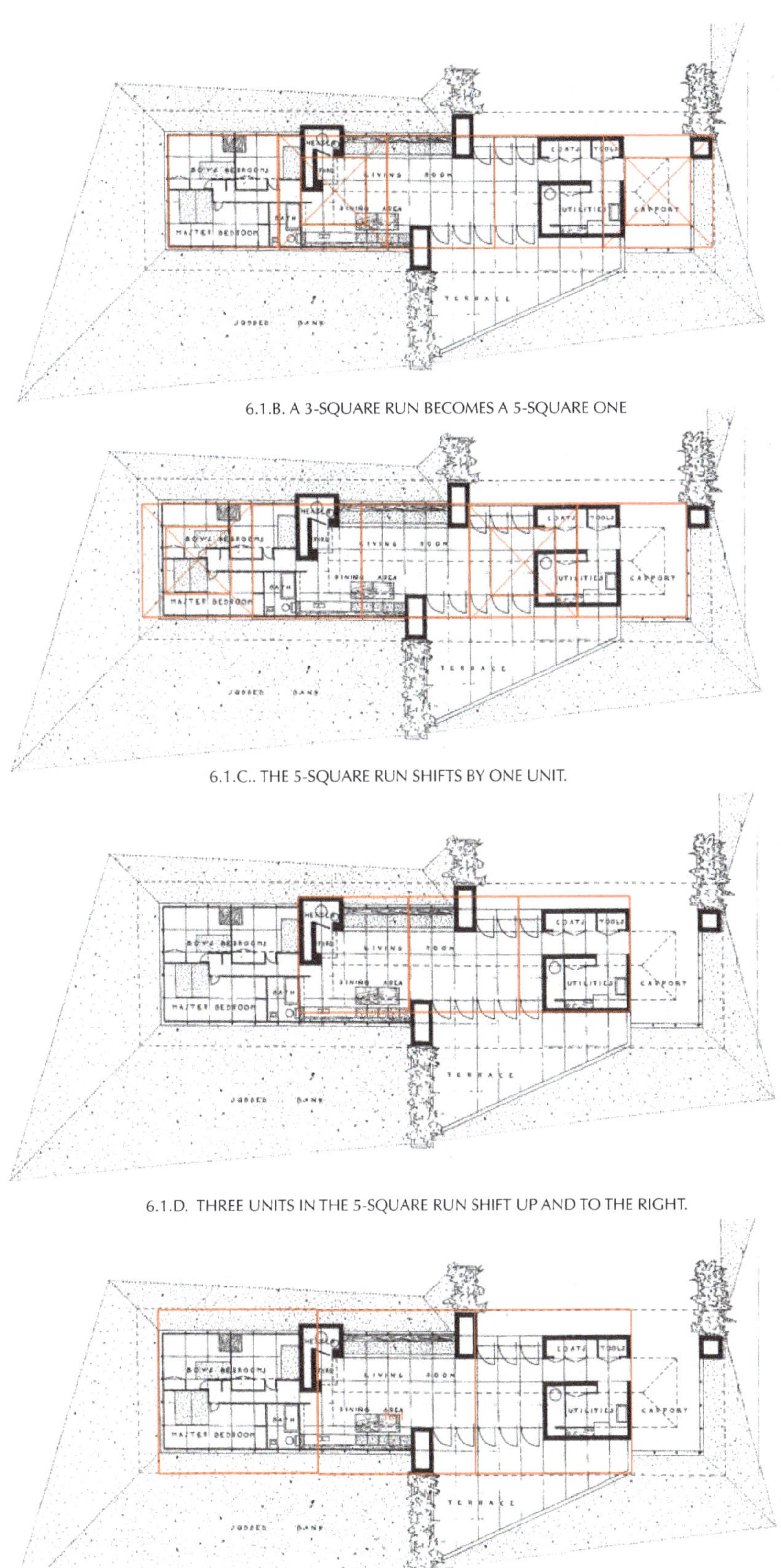

6.1.B. A 3-SQUARE RUN BECOMES A 5-SQUARE ONE

6.1.C.. THE 5-SQUARE RUN SHIFTS BY ONE UNIT.

6.1.D. THREE UNITS IN THE 5-SQUARE RUN SHIFT UP AND TO THE RIGHT.

6.1.E. A 7-UNIT RUN OF THREE ENCOMPASSES THE MAIN BUILDING.

The HERBERT JACOBS HOUSE

Perhaps the most famous of the several hundred Usonian homes is the second designed but the first built, for a journalist, Herbert Jacobs, and his family. Given a corner lot, he generated an L-shaped plan that screened a rear yard and its garden from the street.

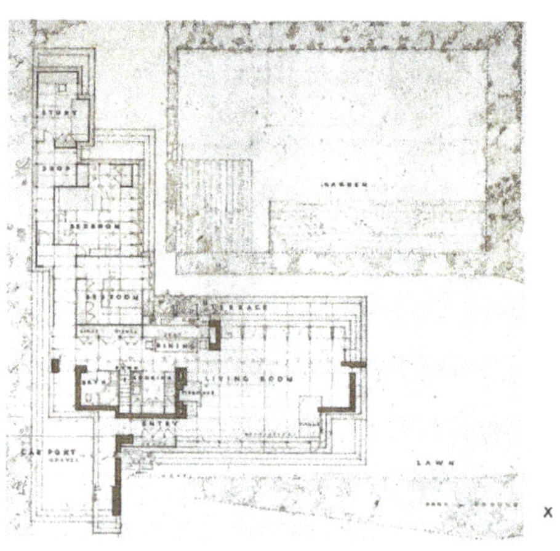

6.2. THE HERBERT JACOBS HOUSE
1936, MADISON, WISCONSIN

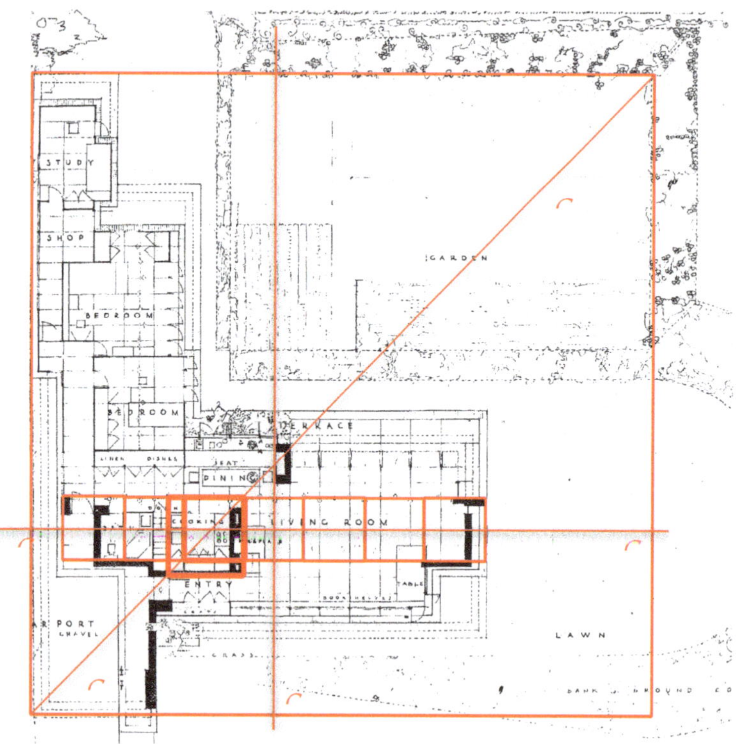

6.2.A THE GERMINAL SQUARES ARE IN BOLD RED.

In one original studio plan, reproduced here, the yard is completed by a perimeter hedge, and the inner face of this hedge completes a perfect square whose other three sides precisely outline the outer faces of the roof. Within the grid of this all-encompassing master square, two nested small squares (bold red) grow off one of its diagonals. A run of seven squares, generated by multiplying horizontally the smaller of the two squares, encompasses the piers at each end. Note how the vertical centerline of this run and the diagonal of the master square fix the location of the free-standing masonry element that terminates the dining alcove. (6.2.A.)

Generated symmetrically about the horizontal axis of this run, a large double-square ties together the lower and right end faces of the living room roof, the upper edge of the terrace, and the indented outside wall of the bedroom wing. The vertical centerline of the seven-square run is also the centerline of this double-square, and as well is also the centerline of the small garden plot outside the master bedroom! An identical third square creates an L of large squares and neatly locates the inner fascia of the master bedroom roof and the interior wall of the study. (6.2.B)

The slightly larger of the original nested squares, 2½ units on a side, forms a run of five squares that encompasses the end walls of the central spine. Three squares at the right end fix the length of the living room. The leftmost square, quintupled vertically, forms the bedroom wing; a sixth square offset to the left outlines the study; and a two square extension at the bottom fixes the face of the entrance porch, marking the farthest reach of the plan. (6.2.C.)

The long axis of this horizontal run is also the centerline of the living room roof. A double-square generated by the outline of the living room roof coincides at its left end with the end of the run. If the square is doubled upward the new square coincides with the outside end wall of the master bedroom. This new L-shaped configuration of squares is closely related to the first L, sharing a grand diagonal. Its vertical centerline also highlights the dining area brick pier, but coincides with its back rather than its face. Thus the masonry element and the flanking centerlines give emphasis and point to each other; such aesthetic economy, so often achieved by Wright in his late works, helps explain their exceptional clarity and vitality. (6.2.D.)

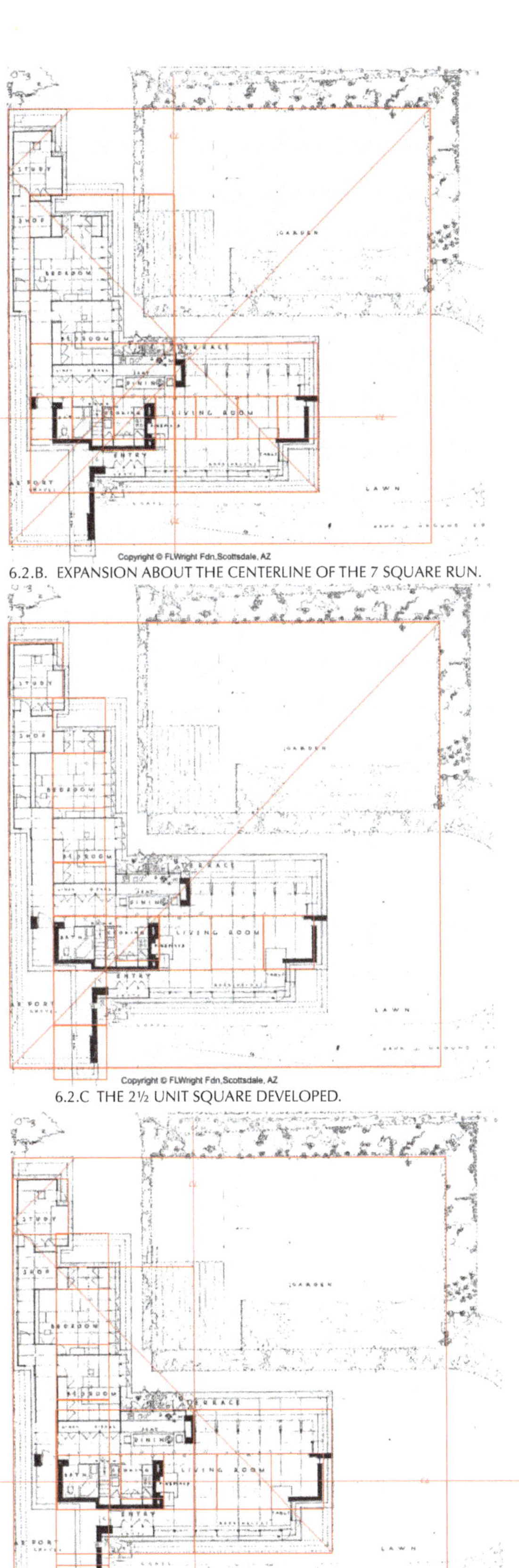

6.2.B. EXPANSION ABOUT THE CENTERLINE OF THE 7 SQUARE RUN.

6.2.C THE 2½ UNIT SQUARE DEVELOPED.

6.2.D. AMPLIFICATION ABOUT THE CL OF THE 2½ UNIT RUNS.

The STANLEY ROSENBAUM HOUSE

Wright repeated the L-shaped theme three years later for the STANLEY ROSENBAUM HOUSE in Florence, Alabama, where he achieved a serenity born of a more thorough integration of its large and small themes. Henry Russell Hitchcock called it "a larger, more perfect version of the Jacobs house."[80] For Robert McCarter, it was "of the later Usonians with L-shaped plans closed to the street...perhaps the most beautiful." [81] The underlying geometry of this home is simpler and more complete than its predecessor: the thoroughness with which all of its elements grow off a common core and are disciplined from its smallest to its largest elements by the symmetries of the square is simply astonishing.

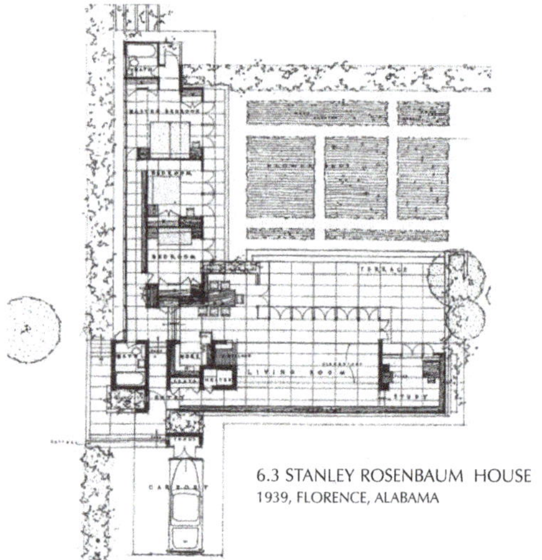

6.3 STANLEY ROSENBAUM HOUSE
1939, FLORENCE, ALABAMA

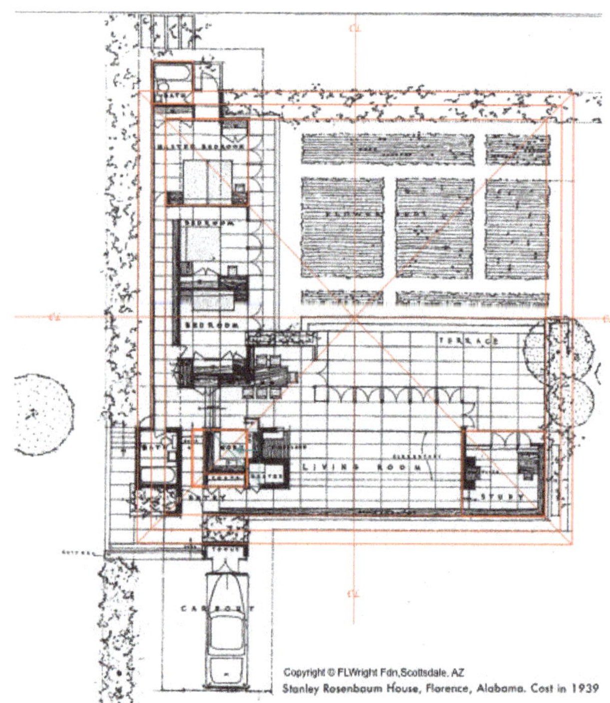

6.3.A. THE PLAN CAN BE GENERATED FROM THE TWO SMALL SQUARES IN BOLD PRINT.

The outside walls of the L-shaped plan coincide with an all-encompassing square, now formed of three concentric squares, ½ unit apart, that relate outside walls, roof lines, bordering hedge, and terrace planter. The edge of the living room terrace coincides with the square's horizontal centerline. In nice counterpoint the master bedroom and the study anchor opposite ends of one of the diagonals. More significantly, at the lower left end of the other diagonal is a nested pair of small squares from which the whole plan can be generated. (6.3.A.)

One of the squares, $1^1/_2$ units on a side, circumscribes the work area; tripled downward, it outlines the tool shed, and continuing downward, a second triplet fixes the end of the carport (and the width of the car, presumably one approved by the architect).

The other original square, 2-units on a side, when quintupled to the right defines the linear space articulated by the two fireplace masses and their connecting clerestory; continuing rightward, two more squares outline the top and side fasciae of the study roof; doubled to the left, the square encompasses the front bathroom

If the 2-unit square is expanded along one diagonal to generate a $2^1/_2$ unit square, and if we multiply this new unit to form a seven square run and offset the 7th to the left, we give definition to three bedrooms and the bathroom and bathroom porch, fixing the vertical limits of the house. At the bottom it locates the face of the tool shed, and this square doubled to the left fixes the outer face and lower step of the entry porch. (6.3.B.)

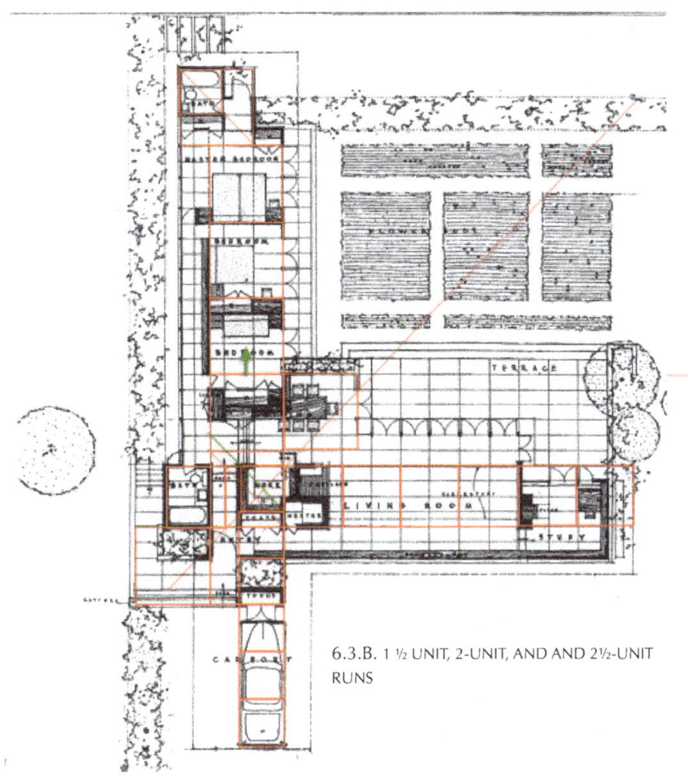

6.3.B. 1 ½ UNIT, 2-UNIT, AND AND 2½-UNIT RUNS

If we were to slide our original $2^1/_2$-unit square up by $^1/_2$ unit, as indicated by the green arrow on the previous image (or get the same result by expanding the original $1^1/_2$-unit workspace square by one unit), we produce a square which generates its own vertical run, one that will be offset by $^1/_2$ unit from the one established previously. The faces of the squares from the two runs, when combined, coincide with all horizontal faces of a series of $^1/_2$ unit-wide, rhythmically spaced elements (tool shed, coat closet, dining area planter, bedroom desk and tables, master bedroom closet) that punctuate the length of the vertical wing of the house. (6.3.C.)

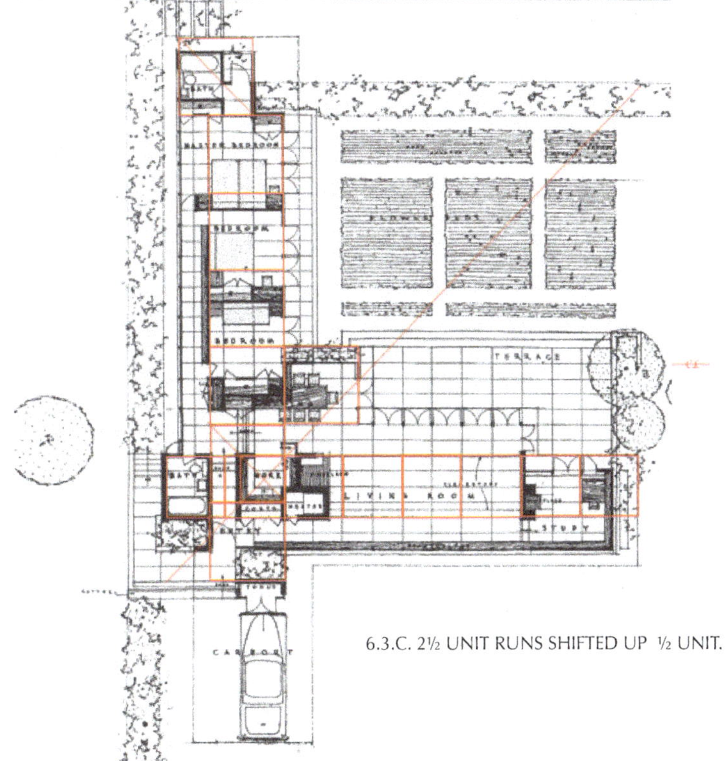

6.3.C. 2½ UNIT RUNS SHIFTED UP ½ UNIT.

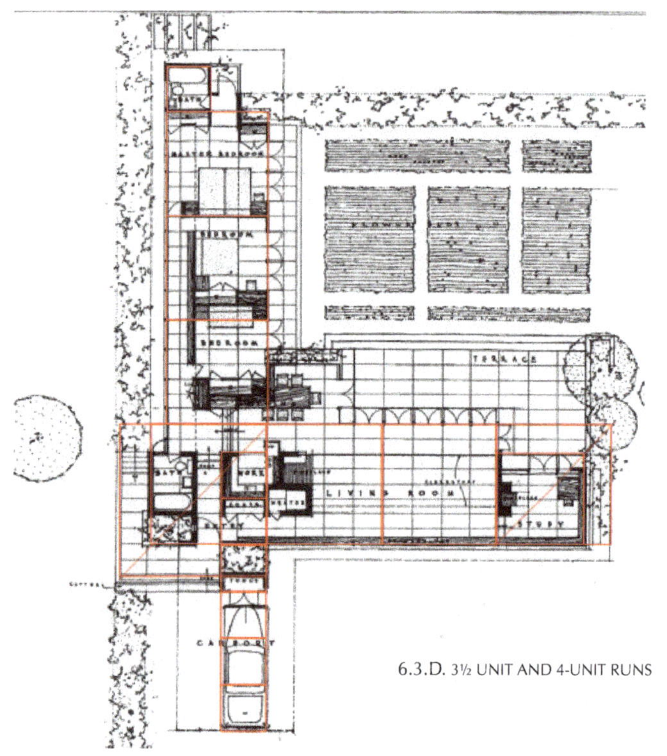

6.3.D. 3½ UNIT AND 4-UNIT RUNS

About one diagonal of this this new 2½-unit square one can generate a larger square, 4 units on a side which can be multiplied horizontally by four. The living and entry spaces are enclosed by three of these 4-unit squares, with the 4th, to the far right, locating the end of the overhanging roof.

Generated about a diagonal of this 4th square, is a 3-unit square that circumscribes the study and its terrace-sheltering roof projection; this is the same square we saw anchoring the bottom right corner of the master square.

Abutting the run of 4-unit squares, a vertical triplet of 3½-unit squares encompasses the bedrooms, topped by a diminished square that outlines the bathroom. (6.3.D.)

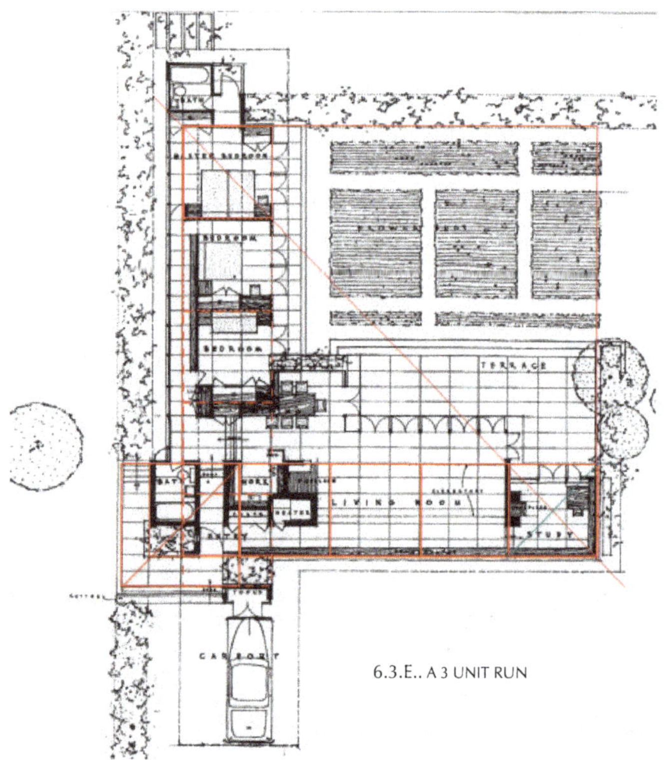

6.3.E.. A 3 UNIT RUN

The 3-unit square circumscribing the study is the rightmost of a run of five that exactly circumscribes the masonry elements that define the lower L of the house. (6.3.E.)

Remarkably, this plan incorporates every unit or ½ unit size between one and four units of length with at least one run that plays a significant role, and every one of them can be generated off the original nested pair. The end result is a work of such thorough integration, resolved in such simple and clear terms, that the home in plan and in exterior massing achieves a serenity and elegance rare even by the master's lofty standards (6.3.E.)

The LOWELL WALTER HOUSE

The elegant plan of the LOWELL WALTER HOUSE of 1945 is generated from a 5'3" unit square repeating vertically and horizontally to "tile" a master square that appears to blossom at the end of the entry/bedroom wing, giving the effect of a flower opening at the end of its stem.

Its main living space is a "garden room" contained within a large square formed by tiling of the central unit of the design grid, a 5'-3" square; this square when tripled in each direction outlines the clerestory lighting at the center of room; this triple-square in turn is tripled in each direction, generating a 9-unit square that locates the perimeter terrace wall. The garden room's all glass exterior walls, located on the centerline of the outer 3-unit squares, form a third ring concentric about the central planter. (6.4.A.)

The true generative heart of the plan is not the central square alone, but a trio of three contiguous 3-unit squares. To the right of the central 3-unit square, a second 3-unit square aligns with a kitchen wall, and generates from one diagonal a 4-unit square that defines a low wall that encloses the dining terrace. (6.4.B) Contiguous to it, a third 3-unit square circumscribes three walls of the kitchen and expands along one of its diagonals to form a larger square that defines the entry porch and roof. (6.4.B). This third 3-unit square also doubles—and its double pivots 30°, slides to the right, and multiplies rightward to form a linear trio which give the outline of the bedroom wing. A run of smaller, 2-unit squares, the width of the bedrooms themselves, begins at the heavy masonry kitchen wall and runs to the far wall of the tool room, anchoring the terminus of the flower's 'stem.'. The fourth square in this series, along one diagonal, generates a larger square that fixes the outline of the master bedroom. Similarly generated is the proposed outline for a maid's room. (6.4.B.)

Three compositional devices have been overlapped to create a plan of gentle movement and pleasing expansiveness: the tiling of the major square into nine 3-unit squares; the linear multiplication of squares to form the bedroom wing; and the expansion of four 3-unit squares along their diagonals. We should notice how the squares expand along different axes to create a rotation, and how the direction of the parallel diagonal expansions that produce the master bedroom and the maid's room stabilize and balance this rotation. Finally, the garden wall extending out to the right that may appear to terminate arbitrarily in fact has its end point and the short return that marks it determined by the plan's hidden geometry: it falls along a line that will be formed if the dining terrace-defining square is doubled rightward and the outer edge of the new square is extended upward.

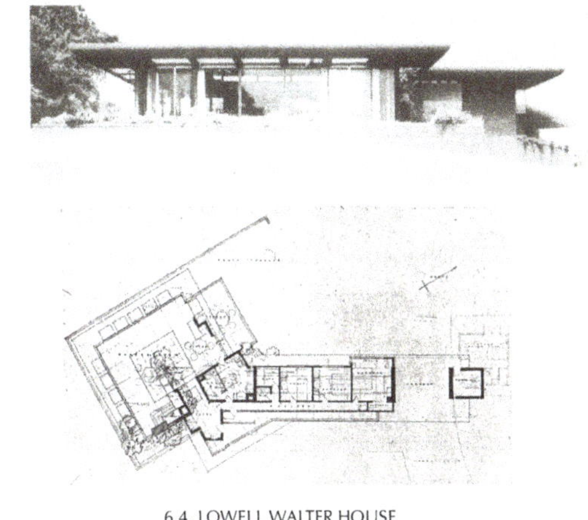

6.4. LOWELL WALTER HOUSE
1945,QUASQUETON, IOWA

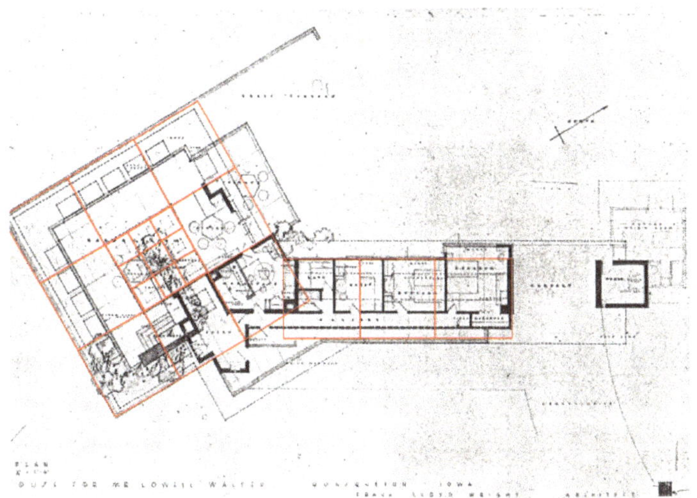

6.4.A THE MAIN SQUARES ARE 5'3" X 3 = 15'9" ON A SIDE.

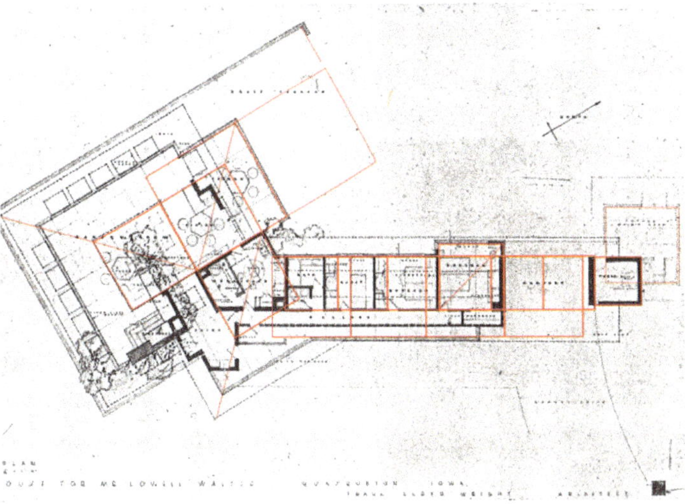

6.4.B. THERE IS A THEME OF LARGER SQUARES GENERATED OFF OF DIAGONALS.

The GREGOR AFFLECK HOUSE

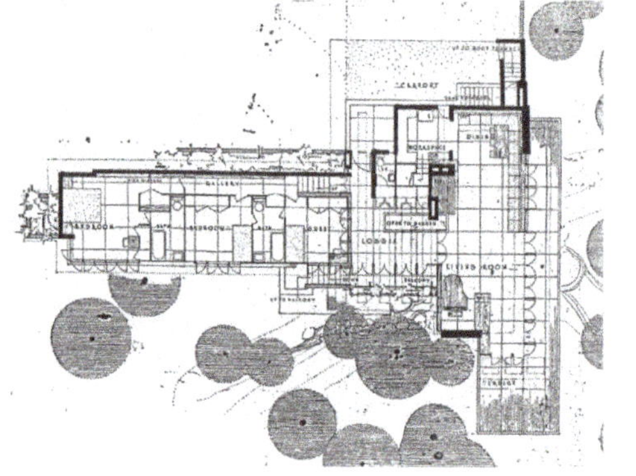

6.5. THE GREGOR AFFLECK HOUSE
1940, BLOOMFIELD HILLS, MICHIGAN

As we saw in the Haynes House, square and linear forms can combine to shape an overall plan; in the resulting composition the linear elements contribute movement and the square, stability. Graceful integration of these forms can be challenging—but with the Gregor Affleck House, Wright made it look easy, generating by strategically overlapped and extended tilings a thorough integration of a linear bedroom wing, a linear terrace, and a large square living and dining space.

Inspired by a sloping site in the wooded ravine of a Detroit suburb, Wright created a partially enclosed entry with a sky-lighted entry loggia that opens to a garden beneath it.

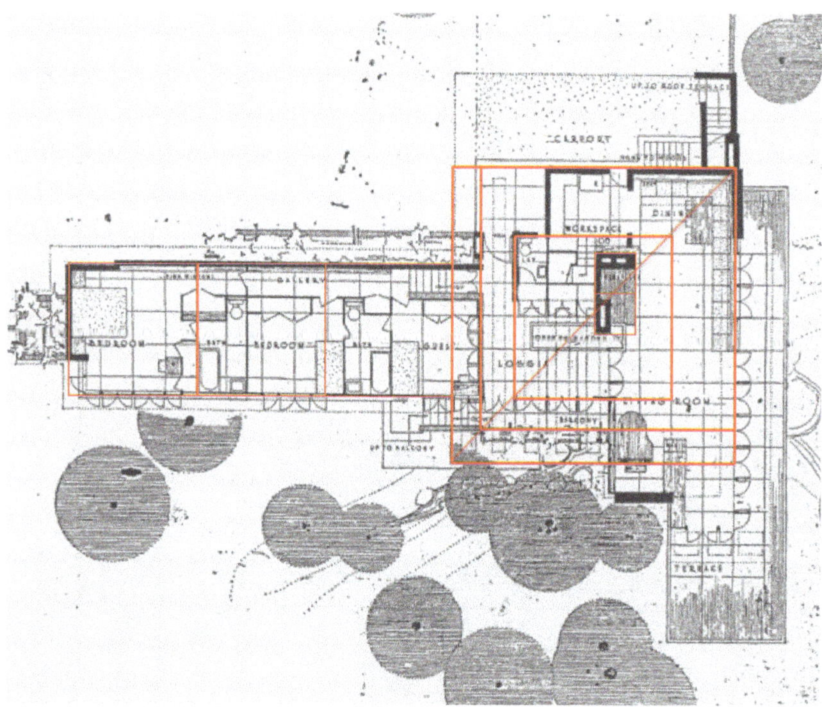

6.5.A THREE NESTED SQUARES MAKE A FOUNDATION FOR THE PLAN

The loggia, a balcony, and the living spaces are related by three nested squares that share a common diagonal.

The inner and outer squares are concentric; the middle square is placed eccentrically between them and shares two sides with the outer square. The outer square is defined by the outside walls at the top and right and by the roof outline at the left and bottom. A trio of 4-unit squares that outlines the bedroom wing abuts its left side.

One unit in from the outer square, the middle square is formed along the entrance porch and guest room wall to the left, and along the inner face of the balcony planter that borders the balcony space at the bottom.

The smallest square, concentric with the outer square, is formed by the L-shaped wall at the entrance and, at the bottom, by the wall of doors opening from the loggia to the balcony. The right side is collinear with the left parapet of the cantilevered end of the terrace.

Notice that the fireplace mass forms a double-square. We will see how it links the development of the larger squares.

The largest square is nine units on a side, and therefore can be divided equally, or "tiled", into nine 3-unit squares. If we do so and then double the top tier of three tiles upward, we outline the carport roof; and one 3-unit tile added at the bottom and shifted one unit to the right precisely outlines the lower terrace roof. But, more remarkably: the middle row, when multiplied leftward by four tiles, at its terminus outlines the brick alcove at the end of the master bedroom. Notice how the fireplace double-square locks onto the upper edge of the middle square. (6.5.B.)

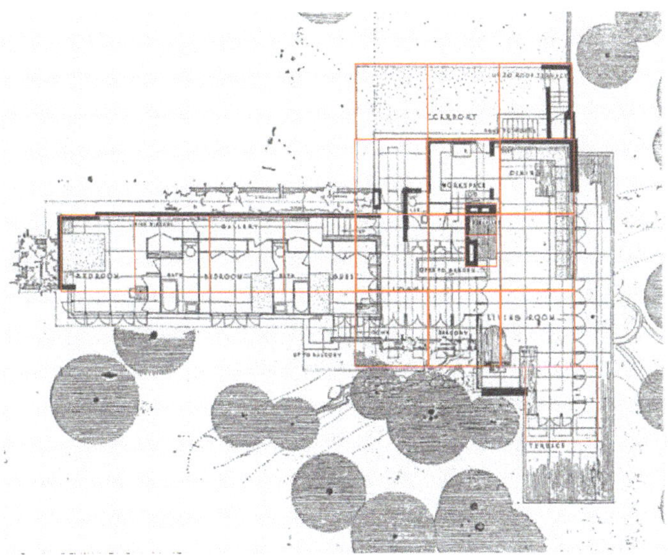

6.5..B. DEVELOPMENT OF THE 1ST SQUARE.

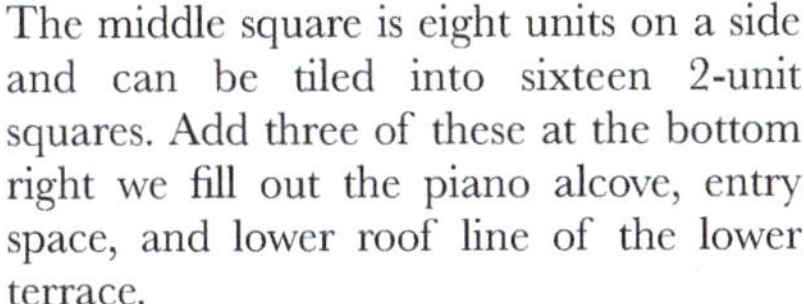

The middle square is eight units on a side and can be tiled into sixteen 2-unit squares. Add three of these at the bottom right we fill out the piano alcove, entry space, and lower roof line of the lower terrace.

If we shift the third row down leftward ½ unit, and add a unit to the right, we locate the terrace parapet, which, we may have noticed by now, is "off the grid." When we then multiply the squares of this row leftward, we find that the twelfth tile perfectly circumscribes the planter at the end of the master bedroom.

Thus we see that each of the width-defining elements of the bedroom wing plays a significant role as the terminus of one of the three overlapping rows that define the wing and integrate it into the main body of the house.

Notice how the fireplace double-square now locks onto the left and top edges of the square in the third from the right square in the shifted run; thus the mass relates the two tilings. (6.5.C.)

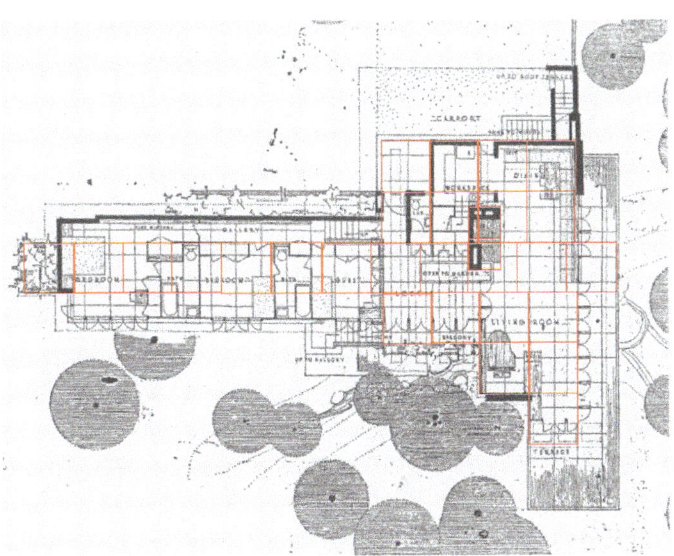

6.5.C. DEVELOPMENT OF THE 2ND SQUARE.

The right side of the innermost of the three central nested squares neatly abuts the two top squares of a four-square run of 3½-unit squares that exactly circumscribes the full terrace. (6.5.D.)

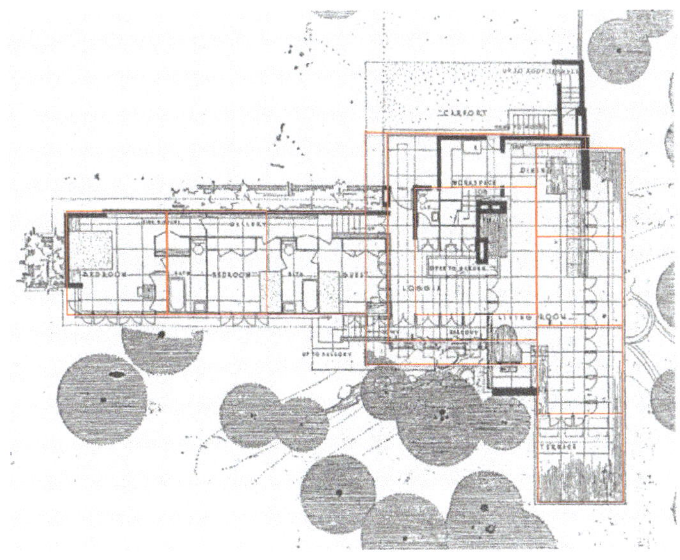

6.5.D. THE 3RD SQUARE LINKS THE TERRACE.

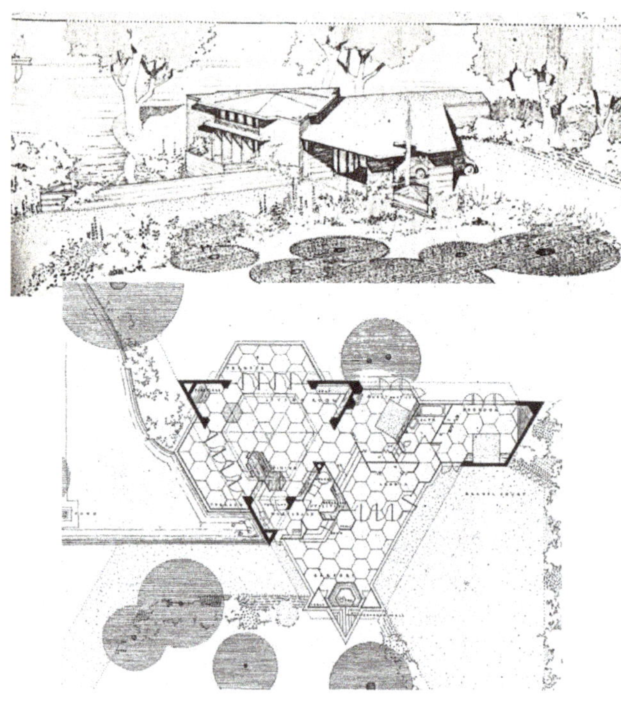

6.6. THE V. C. SUNDT HOUSE PROJECT
1941 MADISON, WISCONSIN

The V. C. SUNDT PROJECT

Wright's method most frequently employed grids of squares or double-squares with the square as prime generator; but it also worked for the other regular and tileable polygons—the equilateral triangle and the hexagon. Mathematically, these two shapes are of the same family: the grid from one may be the base for a plan that becomes dominated by the other. In the V.C. Sundt home project, for example, from a hexagonal grid he generated an extremely clever interplay of concentric triangles. Note that bilateral symmetry continues to be active, but now unfolds about three axes of the triangle rather than four axes of the square.

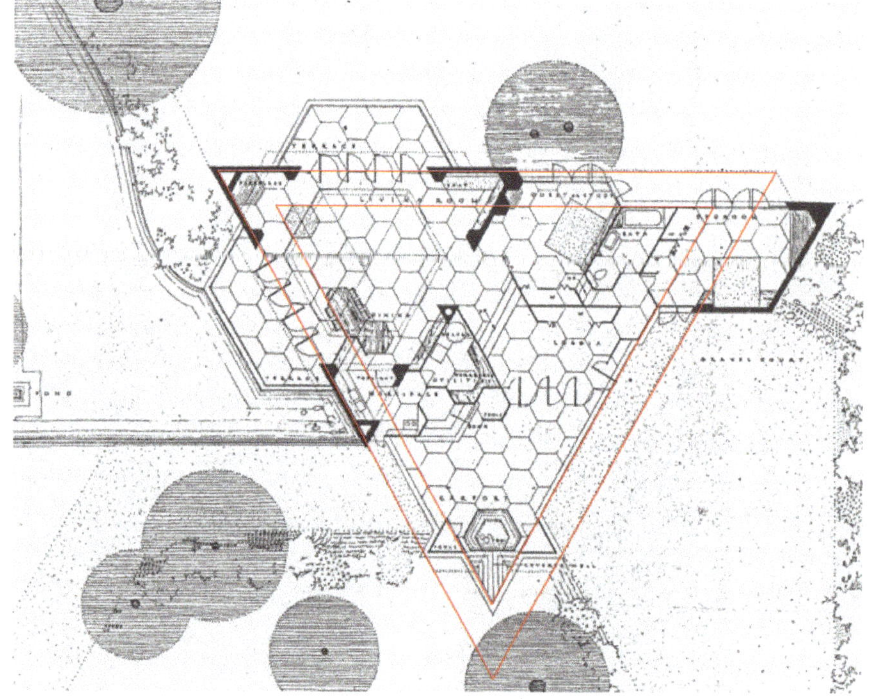

6.6..A. TWO CONCENTRIC TRIANGLES FRAME THE HOUSE

Two large, concentric triangles encompass almost the entire house - the larger defines the two outside walls of the living room and most of the roofline.

The smaller triangle defines an outside master bedroom wall, the entry porch, and in the living room coincides with the long side of the dining table and two faces of the fireplace ottoman.

The smaller triangle is then tiled into sixteen equal triangles, in four rows each way. Extended rightward at the top, this tiling fills out the remainder of the master bedroom, and, expanded at the living room end, it forms two ½ hexagons which, when shifted ½ unit to the left, neatly outline the living room terraces. (6.6.B.)

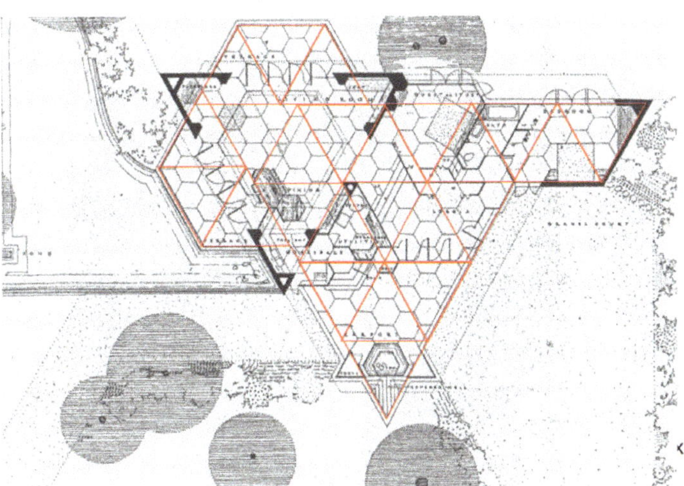

6.6.B. THE SMALLER TRIANGLE IS TILED, AND COMPLETES THE OUTLINE OF THE PLAN

Both of the larger triangles can be subdivided into four equal triangles, the center ones of which are concentric. (6.6.C) Wright cleverly creates the living room out of the interaction between the two large triangles and their quarterings. The room is defined on two sides by the corresponding sides of the large triangle, but the third side corresponds to one side of the central of the four quarters of the smaller large triangle. The slighter larger central triangle of the all-encompassing triangle also plays a role: intruding into the new living room, it clips off the apexes where it overlaps, giving new meaning to those filled-in corners: they are a consequence of the design's generative geometry: they reveal a theme that grows from the very heart of the composition.

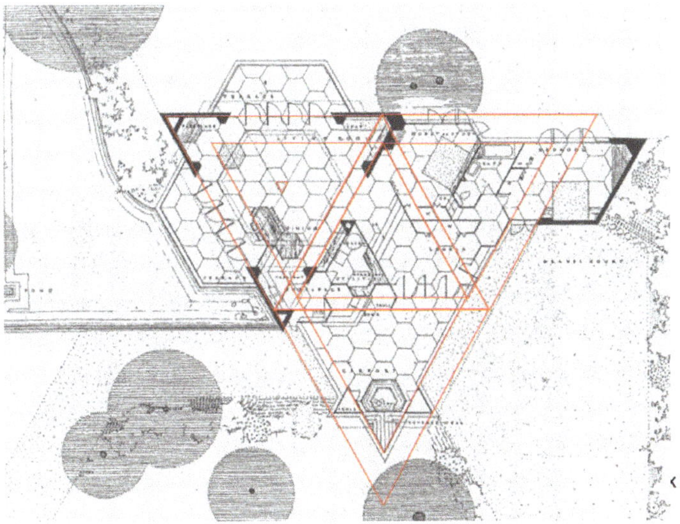

6.6.C. BOTH TRIANGLES ARE QUARTERED, AND THEIR SIDES INTERACT TO SHAPE A NEW SYMMETRY FOR THE LIVING ROOM, TERRACES, AND ENTRY STAIRS.

The hybrid nature of the generative geometry drives the center-point of the living room to the center of a small triangle (highlighted in red, 6.6.C.) that is ⅙th of one of the grid hexagons. Wright made this triangle the common apex of three equal triangles, causing them to truncate each other. (6.6.D.) Opposite this shared apex the base of the lower right triangle coincides with one side of the larger of the two original inner triangles. The bases of all three triangles create the outline of the recessed ceiling.

Mirror-imaging these three triangles outward forms three new triangles whose outer apexes fix the location of the entrance steps and terrace parapets—which, taken together, form the third of the concentric truncated hexagons that are the major theme of the design. (6.6.D.)

In sum, what might appear to be a design of compromises or independent choices, in reality is a tightly integrated compositional tour-de-force. Wright has taken two highly symmetrical, concentric forms—one large equilateral triangle quartered and one slightly smaller triangle, also quartered—and by mediating between their geometries has formed the main theme, the masonry-cornered living room, as a third symmetrical form whose development produces a series of transformations from a grid of hexagons to one of triangles and then from triangles back to a truncated hexagon.

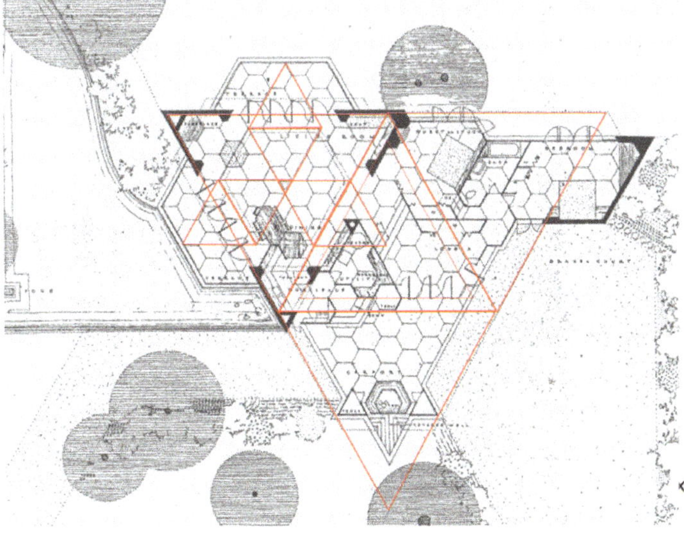

6.6. D. TRIANGLES UNFOLD FROM A NEW CENTER, GENERATING A TRUNCATED HEXAGON.

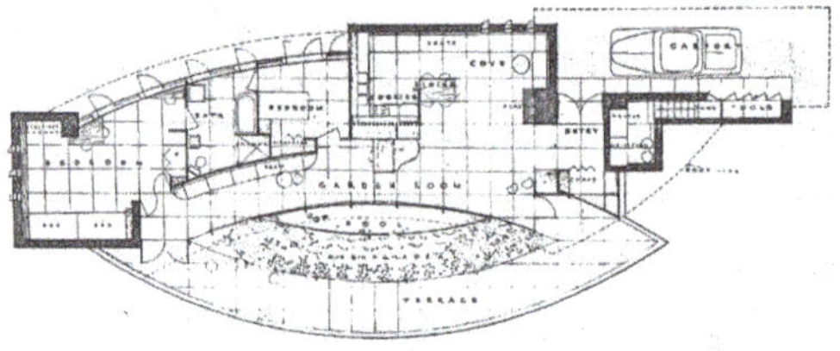

6.7. THE KENNETH LAURENT HOUSE
1949, ROCKFORD, ILLINOIS

The KENNETH LAURENT HOUSE

Curves and circles entered Wright's work in later years, but even in designs where they were dominant square grids continued to provide the foundation for the composition.

The Kenneth Laurent House, considered by Taliesin archivist Bruce Brooks Pfeiffer to be "among Wright's finest residential designs,"[82] is laid out around the elegant intersection of equal arcs, generating what Pfeiffer, adding to the playful Wrightian lexicon, describes as the 'football plan."

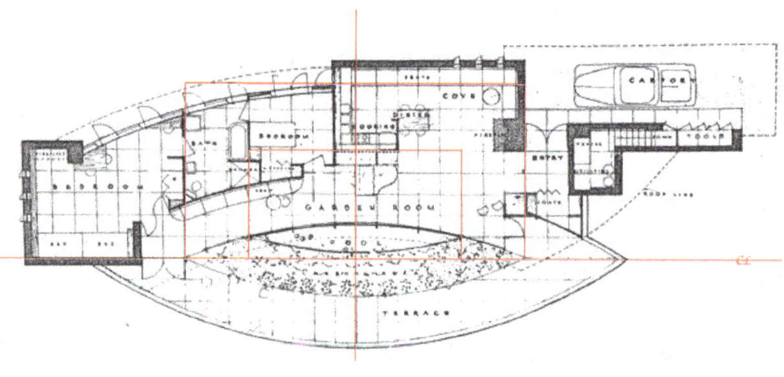

6.7.A. GRID RADIATES SYMMETRICALLY FROM THE INTERSECTION OF ARCS.

The 'football' is bilaterally symmetrical about horizontal and vertical axes, from which radiate a square grid on which the plan is developed.

The plan unfolds bilaterally about the vertical axis, beginning with a nested pair of double-squares; one of 5-unit squares and the other of 8-unit squares, the length of their sides determined by the intersections of the arcs that form the pool and the garden. (6.7.A.)

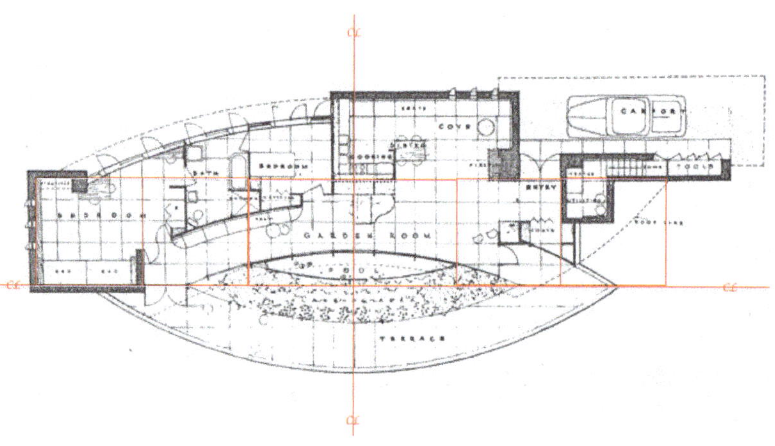

6.7.B. 5-UNIT SQUARES MULTIPLY FROM THE CENTERLINE

The 5-unit squares multiply horizontally. The leftmost of these outlines the strongly stated, brick-lined master bedroom alcove that terminates the left end of the house; to the right, its center emphasized by a concentrically placed square table, one square terminates the right end of the interior, and the final square fixes, at its upper right-hand corner, the meeting of the curved roof with the brick wall of the toolshed. (6.7.B.)

If the rightmost two squares are duplicated above and shifted three units to the right, the new double-square locates the face of the carport roof and the far end of the masonry structure. A pair of 4-unit squares define the kitchen and the cove up to the face of the fireplace. (6.7.C.)

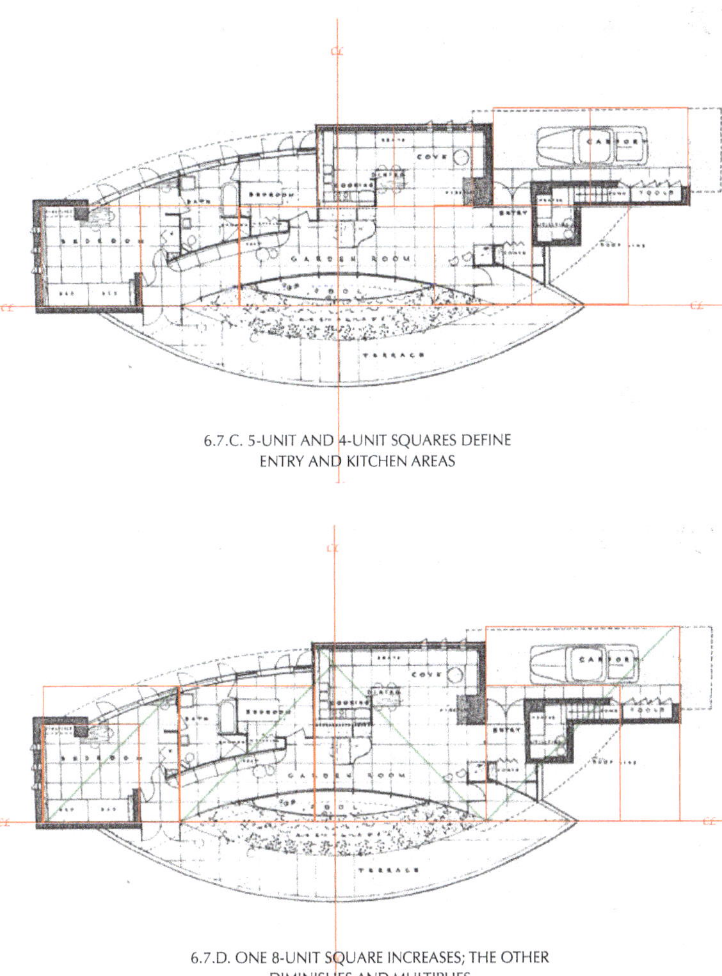

6.7.C. 5-UNIT AND 4-UNIT SQUARES DEFINE ENTRY AND KITCHEN AREAS

Other elements are generated by the asymmetrical and coordinated manipulation of the two 8-unit squares. The right half of this double-square grows by one unit along one of its diagonals to define the full cove and cooking area. By a complementary diminution of the left half, a new smaller 7-unit square now defines the inner bedroom and bathroom. This square doubled completes the geometry to the left end wall, and the new square, when diminished by two units along one of its diagonals, becomes the 5-unit square identified earlier that defines the master bedroom alcove. A third 7-unit square at the right end of the house coincides with the face of the entry porch and its right edge once again fixes the meeting of curved roof and masonry wall. When expanded by three units along one diagonal, it generates a 10-unit square whose top half coincides with the two 5-unit squares previously identified, reinforcing their role in fixing the carport roof face and the terminus of the rhythmic play of the home's masonry elements. (6.7.D.)

6.7.D. ONE 8-UNIT SQUARE INCREASES; THE OTHER DIMINISHES AND MULTIPLIES.

Left unresolved are both ends of the carport roof. These are neatly circumscribed by a triad of slightly larger than 4-unit squares, whose lower face extended becomes the fireplace centerline. This triad abuts the 4-unit double-square circumscribing the cove and kitchen area identified earlier. (6.7. E.)

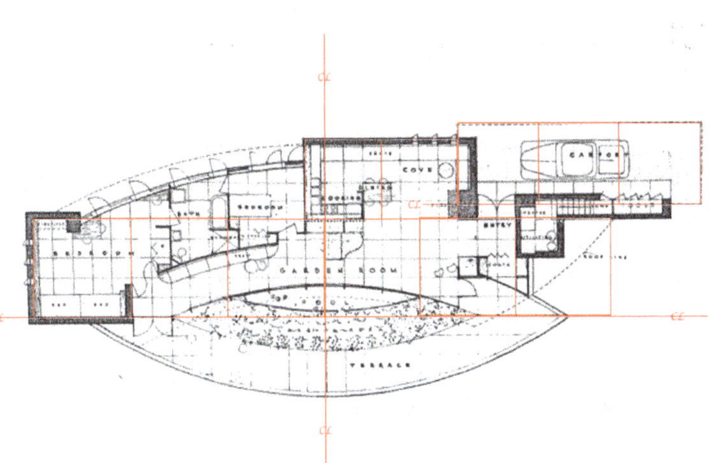

6.7. E. FINALLY, THE CARPORT ROOF IS FULLY DEFINED AND INTEGRATED INTO THE PLAN BY AN OFF-THE-GRID TRIO OF SQUARES.

Even incidental elements—fireplace, entry table, benches, beds, and the piano (whose keyboard is aligned with the vertical centerline) have been incorporated into the formal order, generating a remarkably clean plan that allows the graceful curves to do their magic with clarity and ease.

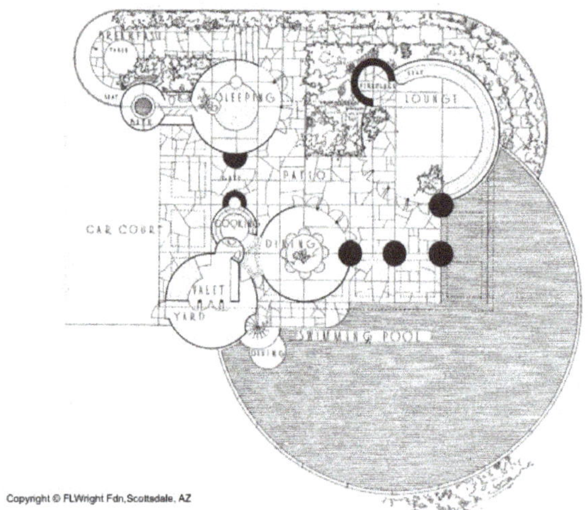

6.8. THE RALPH JESTER HOUSE 1938

The RALPH JESTER HOUSE

In Wright's work, circular themes, despite their often casual appearance, are thoroughly disciplined by underlying symmetrical relationships. The Ralph Jester House, designed for a California client in 1938, but realized 43 years later when Bruce Brooks Pfeiffer built it in the Arizona desert, appears at first to be a free-form grouping of circular rooms about a flagstone patio. Pfeiffer wrote of it that Wright was "Moving again in the direction of freer plan forms,"[83] and indeed the flow of space around the circular rooms is free and relaxed. But here as elsewhere apparent casualness was not casually achieved: the easy manner was hard won through rigorous application of a governing discipline.

6.8. A. A MASTER SQUARE DOMINATES THE COMPOSITION

Although the grid of squares on which the plan is developed would be obscured by the random flagstone paving of the realized home, it is clearly shown on the studio drawing. Somewhat suppressed, however, is the perfect master square, six units on a side that rises from the grid and frames the whole composition. Its perfection is broken only once, and only slightly, on the entrance side; here the paving protrudes beyond the master square, probably deliberately, to enhance the invitation to enter, and is done in a manner that ties the new paving edge to the roof line, which projects beyond the master square by the same small amount.

A little examination reveals that each circle relates to the grid both by its center, which coincides with the intersection of a grid or ½ grid line, and by its circumference, which is always tangent to one of these lines. (6.8.B.) (There are two exceptions to this rule, and they are crafted to interact: the small diameters of the solid piers make tangency of their faces to grid lines impossible, and the center of the largest room, the lounge, lies not on a grid or ½ grid line but on the vertically extended tangent to the inner faces of two of these piers. (6.8.C.))

Within this otherwise rigorous framework Wright skillfully creates balance and rhythm from the wealth of potential relationships between circumferences and centers of adjacent circles. Wright first strengthens the major axes of the large master square. The large garden to the left of the lounge coincides with the master square's vertical and horizontal centerlines as they cross at the square's center, emphasizing both centerlines and the square's center. Centered on the lower end of the vertical axis, the round dining room adds weight and stability to an already stable design. Along one of the master diagonals, two circles, identical in size and in distance from the center, are placed in balanced opposition, like the ends of a barbell. (6.8.B.) These two circles also fall at the exact center of two of the four squares that are formed if we quarter the master square, a quartering emphasized by the placement of the garden.

One theme formed from the relationship between two circles in their largest iteration dominates the composition and is repeated several times at smaller scales, giving to the whole coherence and rhythm: two circles of unequal size, the larger always to the right, are tied together by a unit line tangent to their perimeters. The largest of these pairings, made up of the breakfast patio at the top left end of the terrace and the perimeter garden curving around the lounge to the right, frames the entire upper part of the composition. This pairing is perfectly balanced about the composition's center, due to the careful placement of the lounge, which, as we have noted, is the only circle not centered precisely on a unit or ½ unit line: instead, it is centered on a vertical line tangent to the inner faces of the two piers below it. (6.8.C.) By keeping its center just inside the master square, its much larger size does not overpower the counterbalance provided by the breakfast patio. Echoing this shape and parallel to it are the pairings of the sleeping room and lounge and of the kitchen and dining room. Swung 90° clockwise, the cooking-dining pair matches the cooking-valet pair, so that in total we have four statements of the theme. These add movement and rhythm and, by the dramatic appearance of one of them as the garden wall, closure to the overall composition. (6.8.D.)

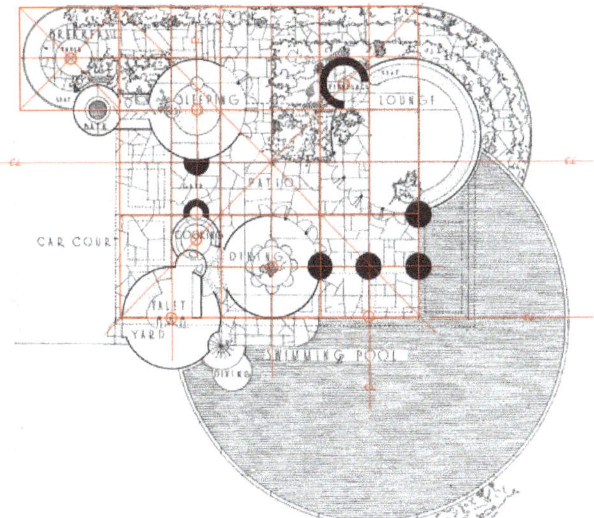

6.8.B. EQUAL SUBDIVISION OF THE MASTER SQUARE CONTROL THE DESIGN

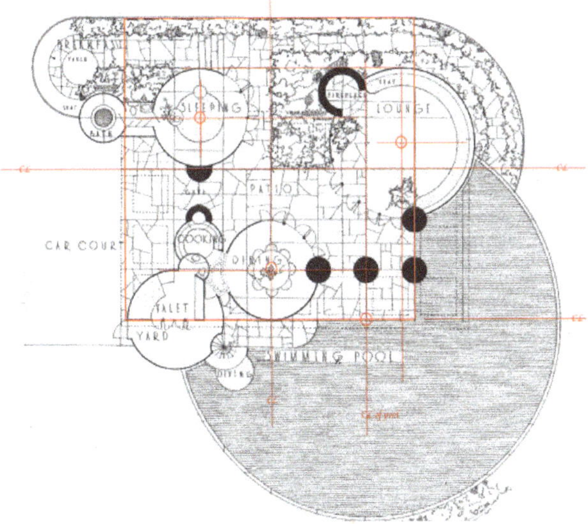

6.8.C. THE TWO OFF-THE-GRID ELEMENTS ARE COORDINATED

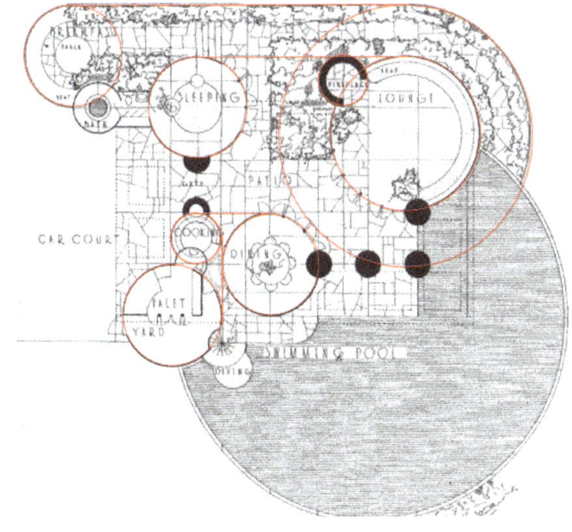

6.8. D. PAIRINGS THAT CREATE A REPEATING THEME

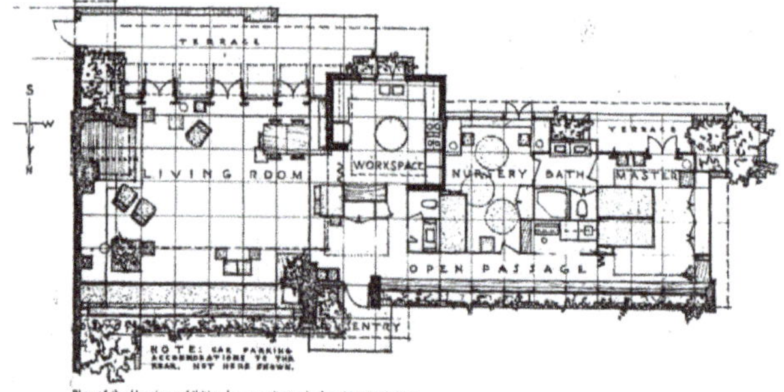

Plan of the Usonian exhibition house as it was built in New York City.

6.9. THE USONIAN EXHIBITION HOUSE 1953

The USONIAN EXHIBITION HOUSE

For a major retrospective at the Museum of Modern Art, Wright produced this demonstration of his mastery of the small home. Here he develops the plan from some of his simplest and most effective manipulations of the square: the bilaterally symmetrical nesting of major squares that announces the major theme of the composition and that anchors it; the runs of squares at several different scales (1½, 3, 4, 5, 6, 7, and 9 units); and the development of closely spaced vertical centerlines.

A living room and terrace are organized within a large square, and a square kitchen ("workspace" on the plan) mediates between it and a pair of squares that form the bedroom wing. (6.9. A.)

Notice how the plan is made even simpler by the theme of square spaces strongly defined but each open at one corner: the fireplace and the workspace, with the open corners of each opening to the living room; and the living room, opening to the workspace and bedroom wing. (6.9. A.)

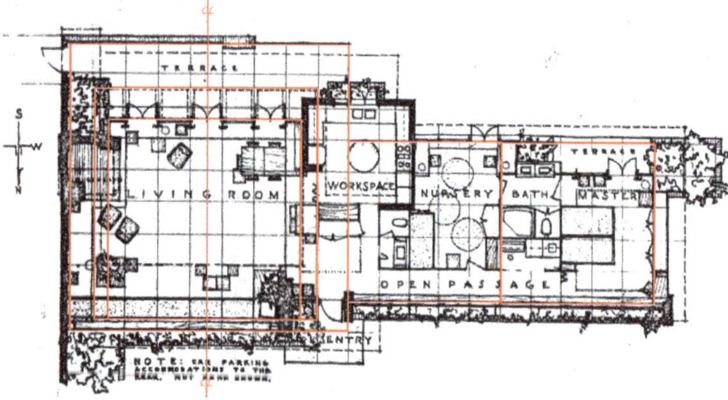

6.9. A. THREE NESTED SQUARES BILATERALLY SYMMETRICAL ABOUT A VERTICAL AXIS ANNOUNCE THE THEME.

Major features of the living area define three large squares, 6, 7, and 9 units on a side nested symmetrically about a common vertical centerline. The bedroom wing is defined by a pair of 5-unit squares adjacent to the 9-unit square, giving us the width of the wing. (6.9. A.)

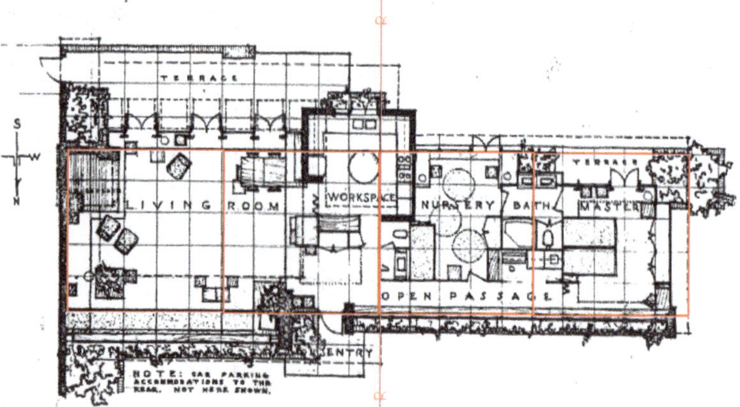

6.9.B. THE BEDROOM SQUARES DOUBLED GIVE THE LENGTH OF THE HOUSE.

If we slide the pair of 5-unit squares one unit to the right and repeat it the left, we have a four 5-unit square run that establishes the length of the house, running from the far living room wall to the face of the roof at the home's right end. Wright makes the vertical centerline of this run coincide with the right edge of the roof over the entry. (6.9. B.)

The run of four 5-unit squares is equal in length to a run of five 4-unit squares, and such a run has been invoked by Wright to separate the open passage from the rooms it serves. (6.9. C.)

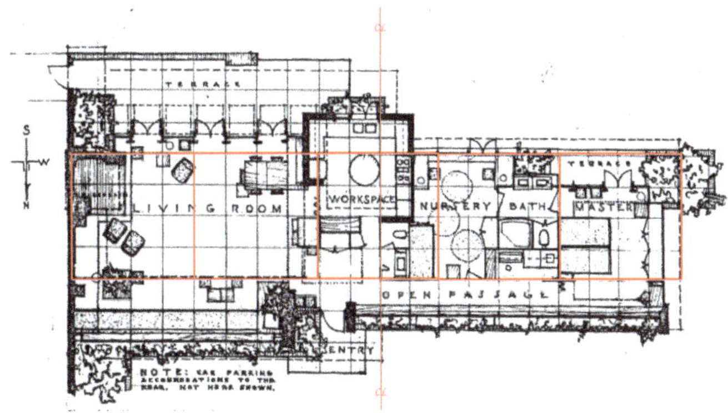

6.9.C. FIVE 4-UNIT SQUARES EQUAL FOUR 5-UNIT SQUARES, AND THE NEW RUN SEPARATES THE OPEN PASSAGE.

Along the same path Wright also generates a run of 3-unit squares, whose top horizontal edge defines the exterior wall of the master bedroom and coincides with the brick return of the left workspace wall. (6.9.D.) The run is further defined along its bottom horizontal by the front edge of the clerestory "shelf" above the built in seat in the living room. This run cannot be the same length as the other two: seven 3-unit squares equal 21 units, not the 20 units of the previous two. But Wright has provided for this: this run carries to the outer face of the planter off the master bedroom, so that the whole run gives us the full length of the house. The vertical centerline of the houses's full length is marked by the right end of the living room roof, and the horizontal centerline is the horizontal centerline for both the living room and the bedroom wing. (6.9.D.)

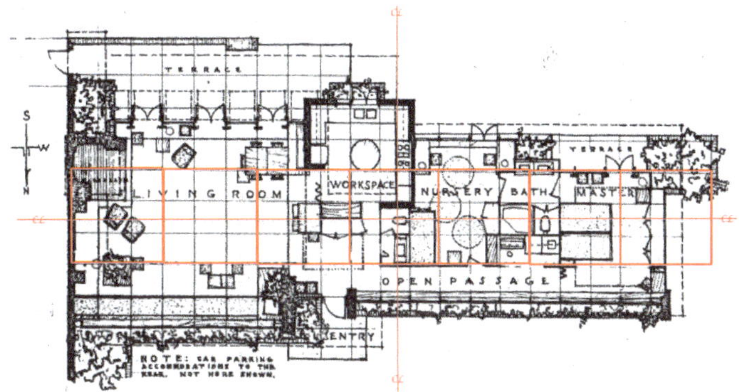

6.9. D. A 3-UNIT RUN FIXES THE END PLANTER, OUTSIDE WALL OF THE MASTER BEDROOM, AND ONE WORKSPACE RETURN

The bedroom planter encloses a $1\frac{1}{2}$ unit square which, when multiplied to become a long run, locks the planter to the fireplace at the other end of the house. (6.9.E.)

This drawing also emphasizes the relationship between the two vertical centerlines. Their proximity gives both life and stability to the composition.

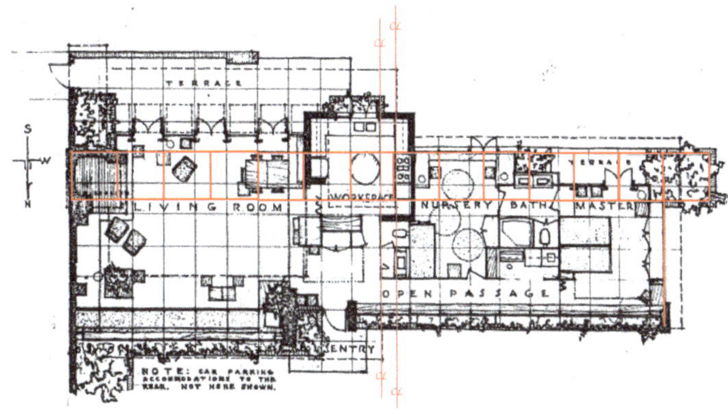

6.9. E. THE RIGHT END PLANTER TERMINATES A RUN THAT BEGINS WITH THE FIREPLACE.

The JORGINE BOOMER HOUSE

In *The Natural House*, Wright dedicated an unusual amount of space to this small but dramatic house. Looking out on the Arizona desert, the angular, jutting cantilevers of its triangular roofs shield the heavy stone walls that anchor them.

The bold penetration of one triangle by another generates considerable drama.

6.10.. THE JORGINE BOOMER DESERT COTTAGE
1952 PHOENIX, ARIZONA

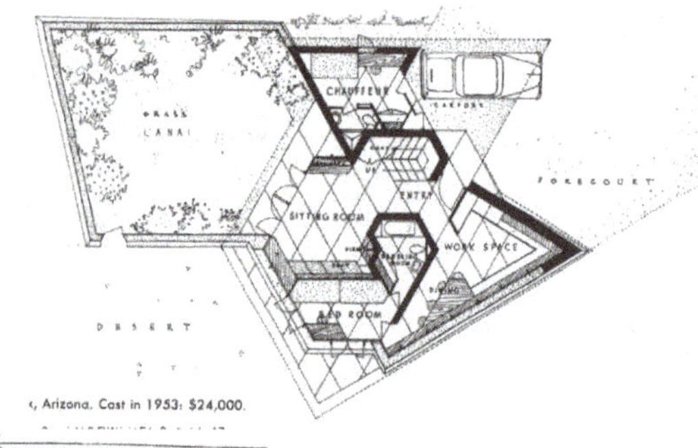

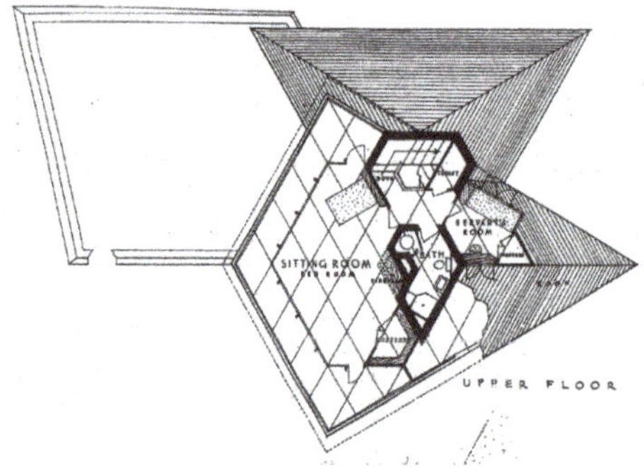

But the drama is generated from the inside out, and its aggressively angular exterior form is generated from a much softer form, a small hexagon that emanates from the intersection of the horizontal axis of the primary (living spaces) triangle and the vertical axis of the secondary (entry and carport) triangle. (6.10.A. and 6.10.B.)

This small hexagon shares its horizontal axis with a hexagon three times its diameter that, thrusting to the left, creates the outside perimeter of the sitting rooms and encourages movement into them. (6.10.A. and 6.1O.B.)

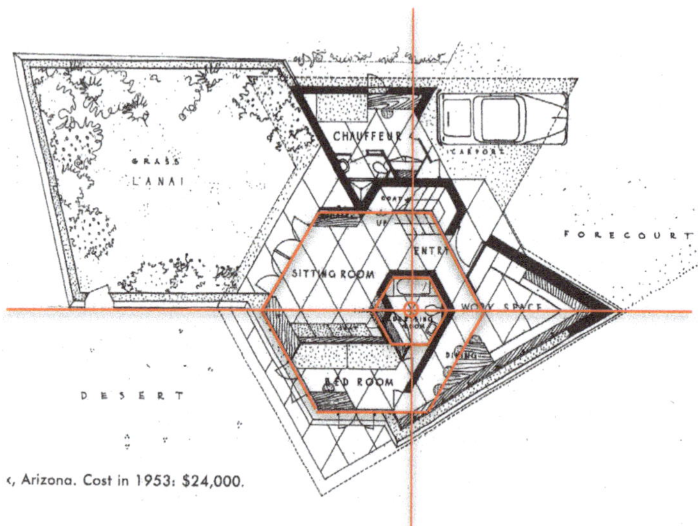

6.10..A. THE PLAN EMANATES FROM A SMALL CENTRAL HEXAGON

Symmetry about the vertical axis of the secondary triangle is reinforced by the symmetrical placement of the double-centered elongated hexagon formed by the stair tower. (6.10.B.)

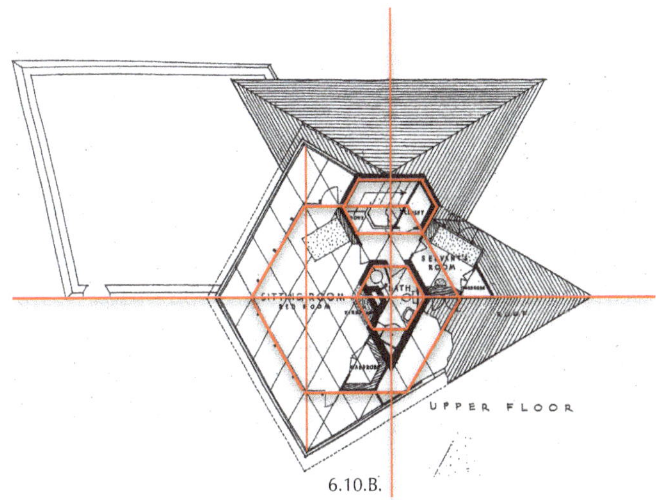

6.10.B.

This larger hexagon at its left end contains a rhombus the width of the upper floor sitting room; and growing concentrically from it a rhombus one unit larger fixes the balcony parapet and defines the sitting room and balcony space. (6.10.C.)

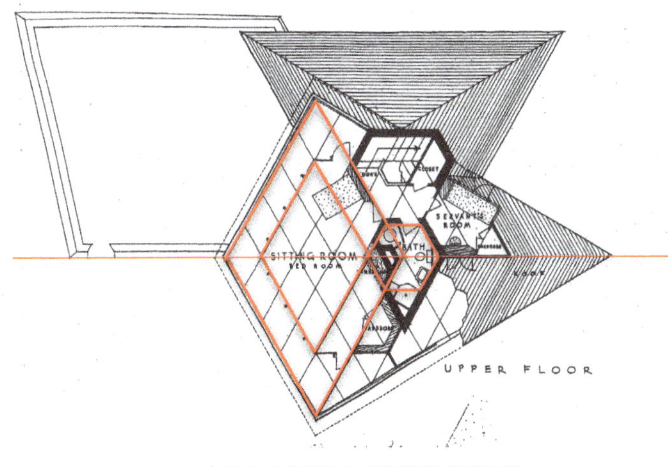

6.10. C. EXPANDING RHOMBUS OUTLINES SITTING ROOM AND PORCH

This larger rhombus, when repeated one unit to the right, ties the roof line to the balcony corners and the sitting room's glass wall. (6.10.D.). Parts of these rhombuses and the larger hexagon combine to give the full outline of the sitting room, making it partake of the dynamics of all three.

Wright's combination of the more comfortable hexagonal shapes for the interior, protected by the more angular, assertive, and protective exterior, is psychologically profound. Probably he saw the affinity of this work to a work he designed much earlier (1896) that also intimately bound triangle and hexagon, a windmill he called "Romeo and Juliet"; but in the Boomer house masculine and feminine are more appropriately related.

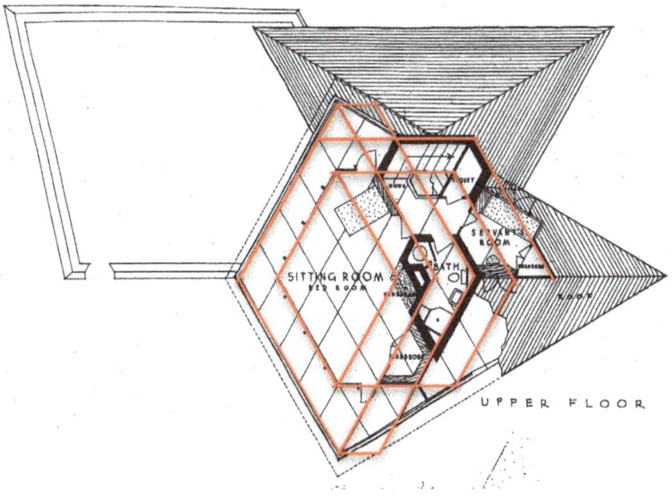

6.10. D. SITTING ROOM FULLY DEFINED

FALLINGWATER

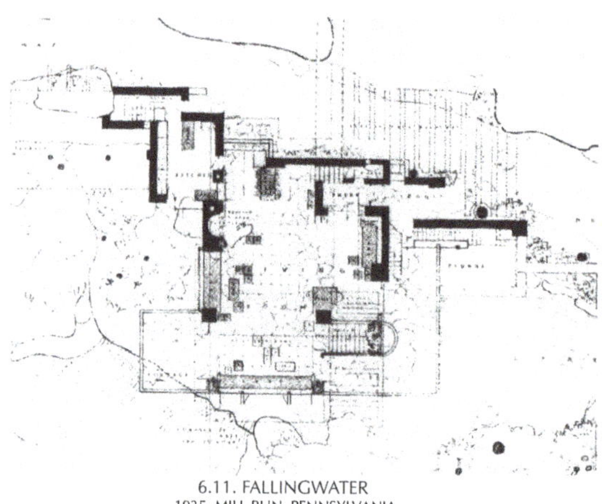

6.11. FALLINGWATER
1935, MILL RUN, PENNSYLVANIA

FALLINGWATER, designed for Pittsburgh department store magnate Edgar Kaufman and his family, is undoubtably the most celebrated modern home anywhere in the world, by any architect. Audaciously engineered to thrust dramatically out over a woodland waterfall, it gets our attention; but more importantly—it is a great work of art.

Below we see the first appearance of the design, in the form of a first draft that is surprisingly complete. It is a testimonial to Mr. Wright's remarkable discipline at work, demonstrating both its rigor and its richness. Already virtually completed in his mind, Wright swiftly put this plan to paper before the astonished eyes of apprentices two hours before the client was expected to arrive for a first viewing. Below left is the first sketch, laid out in pencil showing all three floors superimposed but differentiated by color. Below right is the first floor by itself, redrawn by Wright.

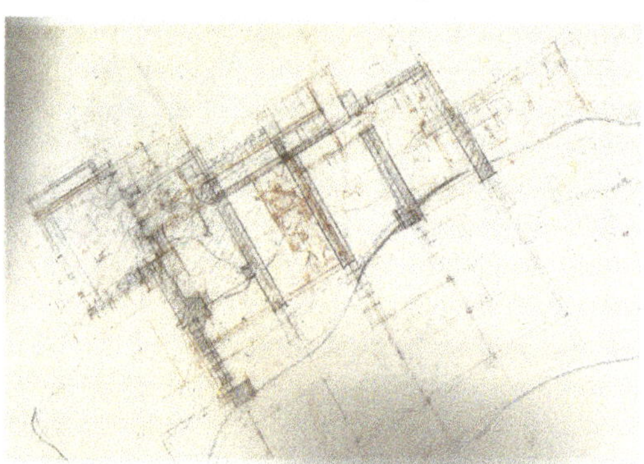

6.11.A. 1ST SKETCH PLAN
THREE FLOORS SUPERIMPOSED

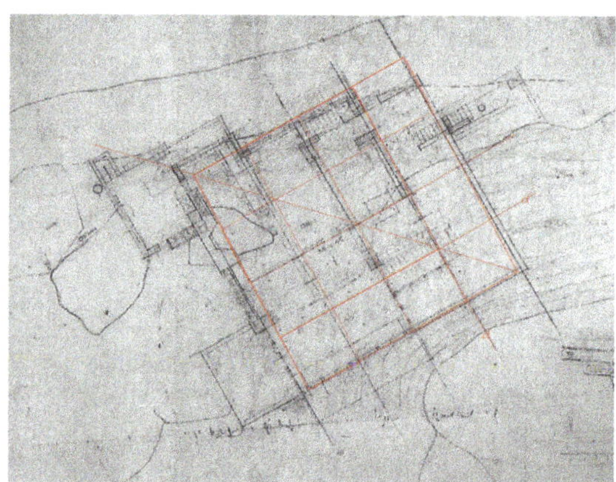

6.11.B 2ND SKETCH PLAN
LIVING -ROOM FLOOR. THE DESIGN IS IN PLACE AND DIMENSIONED

Wright generated a "grid," a tiling four squares on a side. The first four north-south lines locate four parallel piers that support the living space and terraces that cantilever out over the stream. The outer east-west lines locate the back wall, and at the front, the continuous wall that unites the living-room and east and west terraces. The upper two inner lines at the east end pick out the side of a stair and porch; the lower inner line is the centerline for a stair at the right end of the living room descending to the water.

6.11 C. SOUTH ELEVATION
THE FOUR SUPPORTING PIERS CAN BE SEEN BENEATH THE 1ST FLOOR BALCONY/LIVING ROOM WALL

But even more is going on in this "preliminary" plan. Four large squares share one diagonal:

1) The front and side terrace walls define the sides of an all-encompassing large square that takes in the entry loggia and the kitchen. (The fourth side touches nothing for now, but Wright will complete it later, as we shall see in 6.11.E.)

2) Placed within this all-encompassing square is a concentric smaller square that picks out the faces of piers shaping the living room.

3) This inner concentric square shares its top and left sides with a slightly larger square whose right and left sides are centerlines of the outer piers. The right and lower sides of this square meet at a critical intersection—the foot of the stair where it meets the water.

These nested squares form a dynamic quartet: the two concentric squares provide stability; the two additional squares move the composition inexorably in the direction from the anchoring stone hillside toward the water and the waterfall. It is as if the building had tumbled down toward the creek and then been stopped, riveted at, as one critic has put it, "the final link between building and water."

When we now look at the final plan, we find that virtually nothing has been altered, but three things have been added:

1) The largest square had not been defined at its top (north) edge, but a back stairway was added, placed precisely so that it met the back edge of the encompassing square and was itself completed by a double-square.

2) At the client's suggestion, a plunge pool was added on the east side, and Wright completed this with a square, neatly linked to the main body by a regulating line formed from the right angular intersection of two diagonals.

3) Finally, look closely at the stairway to the water (lower right, 6.11.E.): a light well, originally drawn as a double square, is now a semi-circle. Wright has treated the intersection of two sides of one of the largest squares as the center of a circle, giving dramatic point and focus to this climax of the tour through the house down to the water.

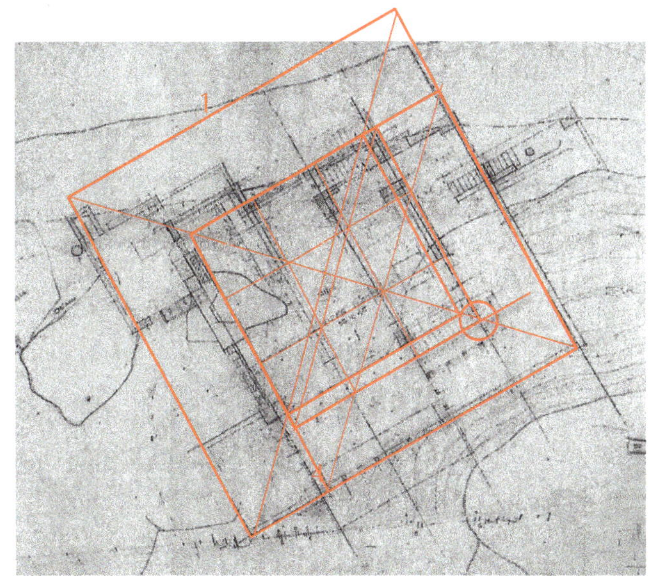

6.11.D. 2ND SKETCH PLAN
FOUR LARGE SQUARES MOVING TOWARD THE WATER

6.11.E. FINAL PLAN, 1ST FLOOR.

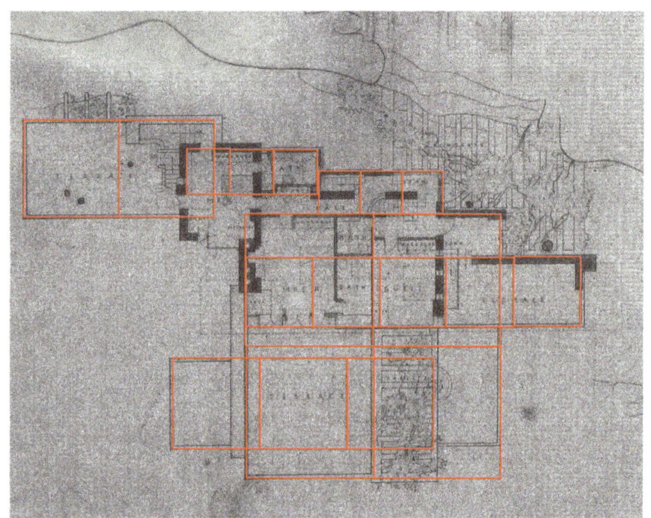

6.11. G. 2ND FLOOR
PROJECTING TERRACES ARE GIVEN THEIR PROPORTIONS AND PLACEMENT BY RUNS OF DOUBLE AND TRIPLE SQUARES

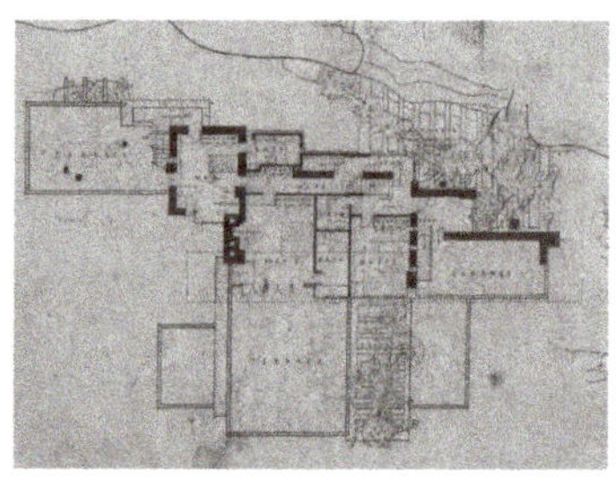

6.11. F. FINAL PLAN, 2ND FLOOR

The multiple terraces, controlled by runs of squares, thrust outward from the stable foundation generated by the composition of nested squares.

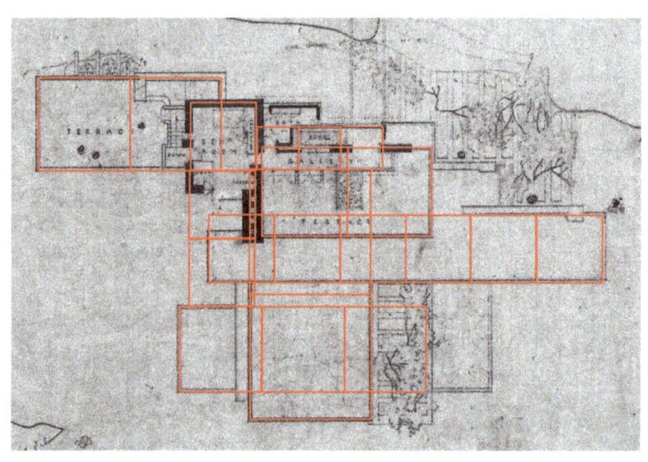

6.11.I. 3RD FLOOR
RUNS OF SQUARES GOVERN HERE .SIZE AND PLACEMENT.

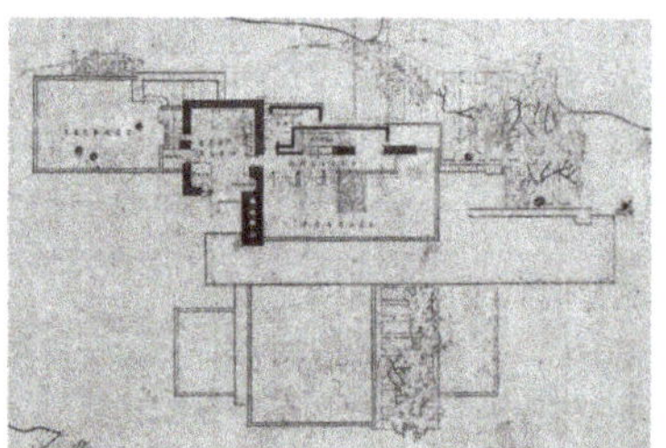

6.11.H. FINAL PLAN, 3RD FLOOR
TRIPLE AND QUINTUPLE RUNS OF SQUARES COMPLETE THE PLAN

FALLINGWATER, as the distinguished scholar Vincent Scully put it, is "rightfully considered one of the complete masterpieces of twentieth-century art." Coming some 30 years after the great ROBIE house, it is dominated by the same powerful combination of thrusting cantilevers and a strong pyramidal base, but here there is not just one but a complex balancing of several cantilevers opposing and crossing one another.

The house is beautifully integrated into what Wright must have considered the building site of a lifetime. Built with stone laid in strata that echo those from which it was quarried, it thrusts out, upward from the woods and stone bank along the stream into the sky overhead and cantilevers dramatically over the waterfall below.

EPILOGUE:

PHYSICS AND METAPHYSICS

> I believe…it to be profoundly true that the inner structure of our intellect reflects the structure of the universe.
>
> Iain McGilchrist

> …the mathematical laws governing nature are the origin of symmetry in nature, the intuitive realization of the idea in the creative artist's mind its origin in art…
>
> Hermann Weyl

Wright's method emerged from the mechanics of human perception, mechanics that evolved from man's immersion in a symmetrical three-dimensional space, its three perpendicular axes articulated and expressed for us, albeit asymmetrically, by gravity. These symmetries shaping our experience are not artifacts of our invention—they are the realities of our world, invoked and impressed upon us by gravity and movement.

It should not surprise us that man's imaginative faculties proceeded his analytical ones in intuiting the fundamental role of symmetries. At the beginnings of Western civilization, at the dawn of belief in rational thought as the means to apprehending our universe, Greek thinkers intuited and came to believe that the universe was ruled by simple geometric forms. For them mathematical ratios were the basis of music and regular polygons shaped the world and the cosmos beyond. Not surprisingly, their architects employed hidden ratios and right angles to govern the design of their temples. From their time up through that of Johannes Kepler (1571-1630), the symmetry of the primary polygons were seen as God or Nature's device for imposing Beauty on His Creation. Kepler himself struggled mightily to retain the circle and the sphere as God's perfect shapes for the orbits of the planets. Overwhelmed by contrary data, through prodigious effort he finally found that at least the orbits of the planets were ellipses—forms of which the circle is a special case—still pure enough, in his belief, to express God's will that His world be beautiful.

But Kepler's laws came to be explained by laws that required recourse neither to God's Will nor to geometric harmony when Isaac Newton (1642-1727) introduced a radically new way of understanding the world. His trilogy of laws relating force, mass, and acceleration constitute a set of abstract entities quantifiable only in relationship to each other. They neither possess nor value any essential visual attributes, and appeared unlikely to yield visual forms whose characteristics, symmetrical or otherwise, might be of interest to the visual artist. Newton's new way of understanding the world came to dominate our conception of what is "real" and led to new sciences that emerged to explore it. Unlike previous cosmologies, Newton's empowers us to remake the world, but confers no honor on efforts to find it beautiful or make it so.

Thus Art and Science became separated, science pursuing pathways to power over nature, art clinging to a desire to bring beauty into the world—but with no foundation in laws conferred by the natural world that would confer meaning or guidance.

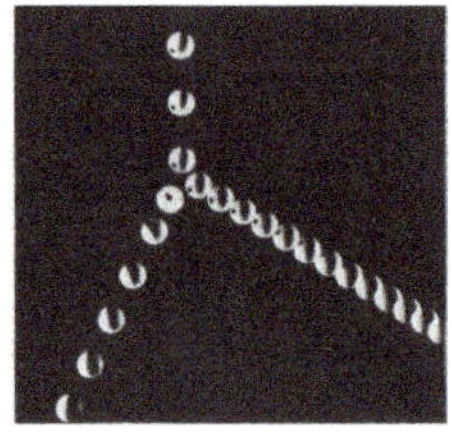

7.1 A CUE BALL

STRIKING A STATIONARY BALL OF THE SAME SIZE.

But in the virtually universal acceptance of Newton's new cosmology, in this world of mass and force containing no obvious visual attributes or visible symmetries of importance, something may have been overlooked. Let us zero in on one point at which truth and beauty parted. Newton's third law asserts that every action is opposed by an equal and opposite reaction. In his major work *Principia,* he presents the law with the example of a horse pulling a boulder: the boulder resists with force equal to the pulling effort of the horse.[84] This creates a collinear pull of one against the other, a one-dimensional event, an event of no particular *visual* interest. But what happens if our force is a push instead of a pull, and the push is delivered eccentrically on the opposing object? Consider a cue ball striking a stationary object ball off-center. The cue ball is deflected but continues and the object ball takes off in another direction. Now we have an event in two dimensions and, surprisingly, our symmetry of force and mass (force times mass before and after the collision remaining the same) now becomes a symmetry of *geometry* as well. The two balls diverge but not arbitrarily: no matter how off-center the collision, the two balls will diverge precisely at right angles to each other. This phenomenon is not confined to the billiards table: protons colliding in a linear accelerator do the same. The phenomenon is a direct consequence of the law of Conservation of Energy and can be demonstrated by a simple proof.[85]

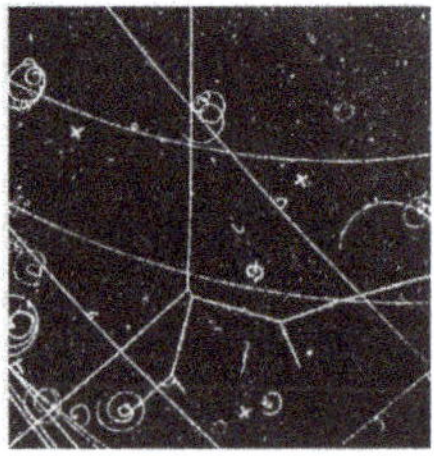

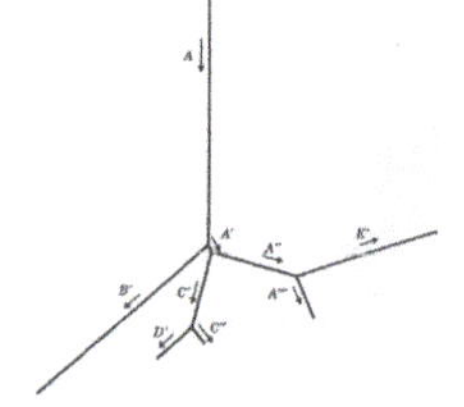

7.2 PROTONS COLLIDING IN A PARTICLE ACCELERATOR.

THE "A" PROTON COLLIDES WITH SEVERAL STATIONARY PROTONS IN SUCCESSION, EACH TIME SEPARATING AT 90°.

Billiard balls cannot take us beyond two dimensions, but rotational motion does; in rotational motion we can see how Newton's laws impose a geometric symmetry on our three-dimensional world as well. Picture a rigid, rotating body. As it rotates, each point in its mass conforms to Newton's first law (the Law of Inertia), and tends to continue in a straight line, but it is successfully restrained by the rigid body, creating a counterforce (centripetal force) which holds it to a constant radius about the center. The momentum of each element attempting to continue in a straight line is constantly at right angles to the radius. Furthermore, in order for this rigid body to revolve freely, unless it is totally without depth (i.e., exists in a theoretical plane of no thickness), it must do so around an axis that is at right angles to the rotation; otherwise, the rotation would bind up immediately. The right angle can be thought of as the body's angle of freedom, which will allow the rotational motion to go on indefinitely. Thus rotational motion creates a three-dimensional orthogonal structure, a Cartesian coordinate system—a system that we may have thought was a mere invention of the human mind.

Likewise, the electromagnetic field has a three-dimensional orthogonal structure. This how the physicist Max Born depicts the relationship between electrical and magnetic forces:

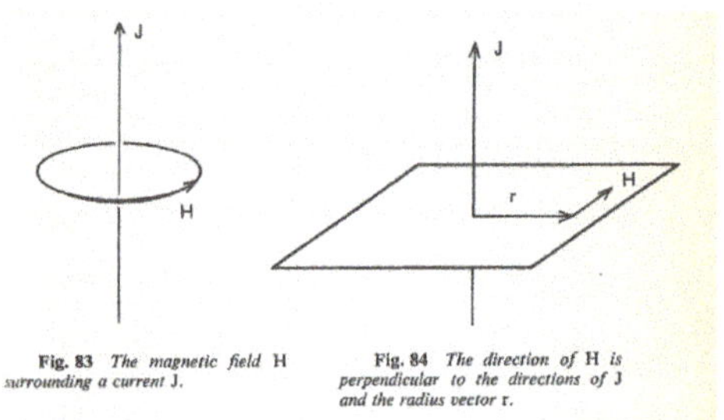

7.3 MAGNETIC AND ELECTRICAL FORCES AS MAX BORN DEPICTS THEM.

Of this relationship he writes:

> ...the effects [of the electromagnetic field] are intimately connected with the structure of Euclidian space; in a certain sense, they furnish us with a natural rectilinear coordinate system.[86]

Magnetic and electric fields, once generated, induce each other in chainlike fashion:

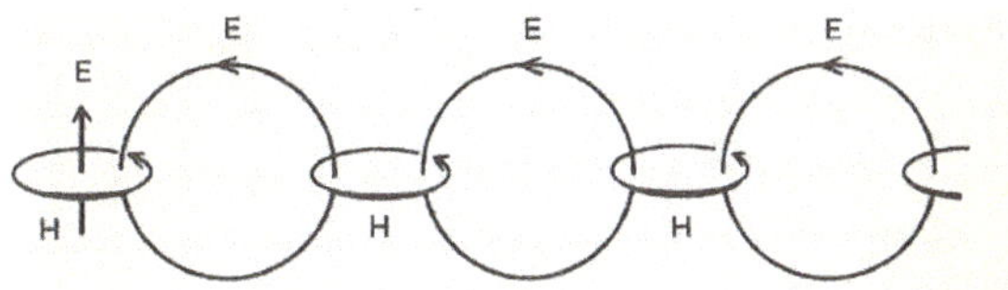

7.4 MAX BORN'S REPRESENTATION OF ELECTRIC AND MAGNETIC FIELDS LINKED BY INDUCTION.

Notice that that the circumference of one enters and leaves the plane of the other at right angles, making the fields perpendicular to each other. This right-angular formation emanates from the very structure of space-time. The field's rigorously orthogonal geometry is an effect of the Lorentz contraction, Einstein's mathematical correction to Newton's incorrect assumption that space and time are absolute. Einstein's Special Theory of Relativity (1905) postulates that a moving body as seen by a stationary observer contracts along the direction of motion; in a moving electrical charge this contraction increases the charge density, which in turn induces a magnetic field. The only direction in which the charge is not compressed is the direction that has no component along its line of movement—that is, the direction perpendicular to its motion—and it is in this direction, precisely at right angles to the movement of electrical charge, that the magnetic field emanates. Thus the very behavior of space-time dictates an orthogonal structure, one that structures the world we inhabit.

7.5. LINDISFARNE ABBEY

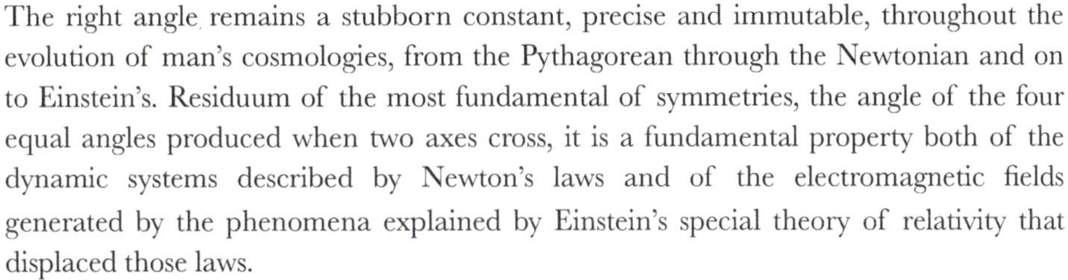

The right angle remains a stubborn constant, precise and immutable, throughout the evolution of man's cosmologies, from the Pythagorean through the Newtonian and on to Einstein's. Residuum of the most fundamental of symmetries, the angle of the four equal angles produced when two axes cross, it is a fundamental property both of the dynamic systems described by Newton's laws and of the electromagnetic fields generated by the phenomena explained by Einstein's special theory of relativity that displaced those laws.

7.6 WINCHESTER CATHEDRAL

Conditioned by their experience of space gravitationally and symmetrically derived, architects for centuries have produced architectural orders responsive to these same laws, and produced symmetries that mirror those from which our physical world took shape. Look, for examples, at the cathedrals and abbeys of the Romanesque Era. Even in ruins, stripped to the bare bones of its form, we see emergent in the remnants of 12th-century Lindisfarne Abbey an order of great simplicity and clarity: round piers and their capitals surround vertical axes from which spring semicircular arches, their springing point coinciding with their tangency to the axes: thus piers and arches are tied together orthogonally, just as are the electric and magnetic fields depicted by Max

Born. Whether left plain, like Lindisfarne Abbey, or embellished by multiple repetitions like Winchester Cathedral; however deployed at different scales and rhythms; and despite the lively imaginations of the many who worked and reworked the form over several centuries, the clean outlines of an orthogonally-related order of interlocking symmetrical forms is always strictly adhered to, ceding little to the clarity of Born's diagrams of electromagnetic fields.

After a 200 years separation by the Gothic period, this order re-emerged, distilled to even greater purity by Filippo Brunelleschi (1377-1446). Its essential features remained the foundation of the clarity and harmony of Italian Renaissance architecture, once again retaining its essential features throughout several subsequent centuries of architectural innovation.

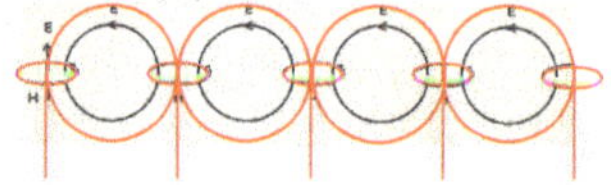

7.7. BRUNELLESCHI'S FOUNDLING HOSPITAL
BEGUN 1419 DEDICATED 1445

THIS WAS THE FIRST CLEAR STATEMENT OF A NEW ARCHITECTURAL ORDER. NOTICE HOW IT RECAPITULATES MAX BORN'S DEPICTION OF AN ELECTROMAGNETIC FIELD.

Frank Lloyd Wright was not the only architect grounded in the deeper patterns that shape us; but he made them the foundations of a method that took him closer to their source, and enabled him to be more fluent, consummate, and versatile than any architect who had come before him.

As we begin to understand how the artist uses the same symmetries that shape the laws that govern our physical world, we can begin to sense that Emerson's insight that "…the truth was in us before it was reflected to us from natural objects" was not the mystical moonshine of a romantic philosophy, but a truth yet to be accorded scientific respectability. At the least, as we move forward in our explorations of how great artists work, and how great art communicates, we can do so knowing that the laws that govern these things and the laws that govern the physical world in which we find ourselves emerge from the same orders, constraints, and avenues of freedom, and that the realms of artistic creativity and scientific research may have more to teach each other than we have heretofore appreciated.

NOTES

[1] *Webster's Third New International Dictionary Unabridged*, Vol. 2. (Chicago: 1 Merriam-Webster 1981).

[2] Frank Lloyd Wright, *An American Architecture* (San Francisco: Pomegranate Communications, Inc., 1955), p. 17.

[3] Ibid., p. 48.

[4] Louis Sullivan, *A System of Architectural Ornament*, "Interlude" between plates 8 and 9.

[5] William Wordsworth, "The Tables Turned", *The Complete Poetical Works*, New York: Bartleby.Com 1999.

[6] Iain McGilchrist, *The Master and his Emissary: the Divided Brain and the Making of the Western World* (New Haven and London: The Yale University Press, 2009), p.232.

[7] In *An Autobiography*, Frank Lloyd Wright gives a moving account of these early years.

[8] Ralph Waldo Emerson, *The Essential Writings of Ralph Waldo Emerson*, ed. by Brooks Atkinson (New York: The Modern Library, 2000), p. 270. Emerson also may have reinforced Wright in his belief in the inherent simplicity of nature and in the mind's ability to divine it: "Nature shows all things formed and bound. The intellect pierces the form, overleaps the wall, detects intrinsic likeness between remote things and reduces all things into a few principles." (Ibid., p. 263-4.) And he may have reinforced Wright's commitment to discipline. (ibid., p. 268.) An excellent guide to Emerson's influence on Wright is found in McCarter's essay "Abstract Essence", pp. 6-21, in *On and By Frank Lloyd Wright: A Primer of Architectural Principles*, Robert McCarter, ed. (London: Phaidon Press Limited, 2005)

[9] Frank Lloyd Wright, *An American Architecture* (San Francisco: Pomegranate Communications, Inc., 1955), p 26.

[10] Ibid., p. 48.

[11] Ibid., p. 48.

[12] The Golden Section can be constructed geometrically by drawing a square, and with the half way point on the base of the square as a center, swinging a radius from a top corner of the square to its baseline. The ratio of the length of the newly extended baseline to the height of the square will be the ratio of the golden section (ø). If the top edge of the square is equally extended, and if a vertical line joins it to the extended baseline, the rectangle formed will be a golden section rectangle, as will be the smaller, vertical rectangle contained within it. If we set the height of the square at 2, we will see by inspection that $ø = (1 + \sqrt{5})/2 = 1.6180\ldots$ This is also the solution to the equation: $A/B = B/A+B$, from whence ø derives many of its remarkable properties.

The Fibonacci Series is formed by beginning with the successive integers 0 and 1 and adding them to get the next term. Repeating the operation gives the series 0,1,1,2,3,5,8,13,21,34...etc.; as adjacent pairs approach infinity, their ratio (larger term divided by the previous term) approaches precisely the Golden Section, ø, or 1.6180... (The reciprocal, smaller term divided by the succeeding term., gives ø – unity, or .618...)

[13] Le Corbusier, *Towards a New Architecture* (New York: Dover Publications, Inc., 1986), p 77.

[14] Le Corbusier, *The Modular* (*Cambridge*, Mass.: The MIT Press, 1954), p. 34.
The original french: "Le tracé, sur plan d'equilibre géometrique, ne vient que mettre de l'ordre, de la clarité, accomplissant ou réclamant une véritable purification." *Le Modulor* Le Corbusier, Basel, Boston, Berlin: Birkhäuser, 2000.

[15] Frank Lloyd Wright, "The Logic of the Plan", *Frank Lloyd Wright Collected Writings, Vol. One*, op.cit., p.249. Also in *On and By Frank Lloyd Wright*, op.cit. p. 345. First published in *Architectural Record*, January 1928.

[16] Byrne, "On Frank Lloyd Wright and His Atelier", *AIA Journal 39* (June 1963), p. 110. As reprinted in Donald Hoffmann, *Frank Lloyd Wright's Robie House* (New York, Dover Publications, Inc., 1984), p. 27.

[17] Le Corbusier 1986, op. cit., pg. 79.

[18] Frank Lloyd Wright, "The Logic of the Plan", op. cit., p. 345.

[19] Henry Klumb, in a letter of September 30, 1980, as quoted in *Frank Lloyd Wright's Robie House*, op.cit., p. 27. Mr. Klumb's full account of the origins of the drawing and its impact are worth recounting:
Assembled and sitting with F.Ll.W. around a fire in the studio one winter day in 1929, discussing this and other matters of 'Organic Architecture,' I suggested that we might try to reduce his delicate renderings of

his best-known buildings to a two-dimensional black-onwhite graphic presentation 'Modern Architects' were addicted to. His answer: *'Do it.'* [Takehiko] Okami and I went to work and produced several, including in addition to the Robie House (drawn by myself) the Winslow House, Yahara Boat Club, Bock Atelier, Unity temple, and the Larkin Building. All were drawn in ink on roll-up window shades…even the stark graphic black-on-white presentations did not produce a two-dimensional effect, rather emphasized the depth of his poetry and the power of the third dimension. Nothing 'International Architecture' had to show could equal it."

[20] *The Work of Frank Lloyd Wright*, Wendingen 1925, reprint, New York: Horizon Press, 1965), p. 57. As quoted by Kenneth Frampton, "The Text-Tile Tectonic," *On and By Frank Lloyd Wright*, op. cit., p. 170.

[21] Ibid., p. 57

[22] Henry Russell Hitchcock, *In the Nature of Materials*, Figures 376, 377, 378.

[23] Rudolf Arnheim, Art and Visual Perception: the New Version 1974, p. 16.

[24] Louis H. Sullivan, *A System of Architectural Ornament*, Plate Three. The drawing of squares is from Plate One.

[25] Frank Lloyd Wright, *Architectural Record*, March 1908; reprinted in An American Architecture, p. 52.

[26] Irvin Rock, *Perception*. New York: Scientific American Library 1984, p. 71.

[27] David Marr, *Vision*. New York: W.H.Freeman and Co., 1982, p. 297.

[28] Steven Pinker, *How the Mind Works*. New. York: The MIT Press, 1985, p. 253.

[29] Arnheim 1974, op. cit., p. 53.

[30] Ibid., p. 248.

[31] Semir Zeki, *Inner Vision: An Exploration of Art and the Brain*, New York: Oxford University Press, 1999, p. 111.

[32] Frank Lloyd Wright, *Frank Lloyd Wright: Writings and Buildings*, New York: The World Publishing Co., p. 250.

[33] Frank Lloyd Wright, *An American Architecture*, op. cit. pg. 54.

[34] Frank Wilczek, *A Beautiful Question*. New York: Penguin Press, 2015.

[35] Since Marr develops his theory out of an analysis of operations the mind must perform in order to experience coherent and correct vision, the reader will be quite right to ask what evidence exists that the brain has the necessary neurological resources to do so. The essential building blocks for such a capability were in fact discovered in the 1958 by David Hubel and Torsten Weisel, who found neurons that were sensitive to lines of specific orientations, grouped so that all angular orientations could be registered. How they are assembled to form coherent shapes is yet to be discovered, but the brain's considerable neuronal resources should be up to the task; for visual processing alone over 100 million neurons are available, each capable of making thousands of connections.

It may be useful to distinguish between researchers of the brain like Hubel and Weisel who explore directly the brain's neurological resources; researchers from Artificial Intelligence like Marr who analyze the logical requirements that must be met to experience coherent images; and those psychologists like Arnheim, Rock, and Biederman, who through experiments with subjects or analysis of art explore what we see and how we see it. In the current environment of inquiry, all three play essential and complementary roles.

[36] The mathematically regular polygons have equal sides and equal angles. Wright employed the three—hexagon, equilateral triangle, and square that are tileable—i.e., extendible as grids without gaps.

[37] David Marr, op. cit., p. 299.

[38] Ibid., p. 303.

[39] Ibid., p. 306.

[40] Wright, *An American Architecture*, op. cit., p. 47.

[41] Irving Biederman, "Visual Object Recognition", *Visual Cognition: An Invitation to Cognitive Science, 2nd Edition*, pp. 121-163. Geon drawing on p.140.

[42] Paul Cézanne, *Conversations with Cézanne*, Ed. Michael Doran, University of California Press, 2001, p. 39.

[43] Le Corbusier 1986, op. cit., p. 29
Le Corbusier, *Vers Une Architecture*, Champs Arts, Flammarion, Paris 1995: "…les cubes, les cônes, les sphères, les cylindres ou les pyramides sont les grandes formes primaires que la lumière révèle bien; l'image nous en est nette et tangible, sans ambiguïté. C'est pour cela que ce sont *de belles formes les plus belles formes*. Toute le monde est d'accord en cela, l'enfant, le sauvage et le métaphysicien." pg. 16.

[44] A *right* circular cylinder is a circular cylinder whose central axis is perpendicular to the two circles that form its base and top.

[45] Marr, op. cit., p. 308.

[46] Dehaene, Stanislav, *The Number Sense*, Oxford and New York: Oxford University Press, 2009, p. 68.

[47] Paul Cézanne, *The Letters of Paul Cézanne*, Ed. Alex Danchev, Los Angeles: The J. Paul Getty Museum, 2013, p. 154.

[48] Emile Bernard, *Conversations with Cézanne*, op. cit., p. 38.

[49] Kakuzo Okakura, *The book of Tea*, Tokyo, New York, London: Kodansha International, 49 p. 60.
It should be pointed out that the incompleteness of the Chinese and of their later Japanese followers is of a somewhat different order than that of the incomplete triangle. In the oriental landscapes, stretches of the painting are empty but suggestive of elements, perhaps shrouded in mist, to be completed by the imagination. This occurs *after* the beholder has apprehended the image. The Kanizsa triangle is completed involuntarily by the beholder as part of the process by which his mind organizes and recognizes the image.

The distinction to be made here is between *preconscious completion* and *completion after the image has been formed and apprehended* by the viewer. The completion called upon by the oriental works follows from the very elusive presentation of elements, and includes (I think) both preconscious activity directing the beholder's attention to the unfinished areas and to the conscious activity of completion itself.

At even another level some critics and psychologists (Zeki, Kandel) argue that the enigmatic smile of the *Mona Lisa* and the elusive expression of Vermeer's *Girl with a Pearl Earring* constitute an incompleteness that draw the viewer into active participation as an interpreter.

Interestingly enough, for every level, its proponents argue that incompleteness invokes the active involvement of the beholder, and that the beholder's involvement helps the work achieve its greatness; yet the satisfactions to be gained are not of the same order.

[50] Ibid., p. 84.

[51] Vincent Scully, *Modern Architecture*, New York: Horizon Press, p. 16.

[52] Frank Lloyd Wright, *The Future of Architecture*, New York: Horizon Press, p. 290. Also in *An American Architecture*, p. 45.

[53] Frank Lloyd Wright, "The Logic of the Plan", op. cit., p. 345.

[54] Le Corbusier, *Towards a New Architecture*, New York: Frederick A. Praeger, 1946-1959, p. 45-6.

[55] Suzanne Langer, *Mind: An Essay on Human Feeling*. Baltimore: The John Hopkns Press, 1967, p. 125.

[56] D'Arcy Wentworth Thompson, *On Growth and Form*, Vol. I, p. 67.

[57] Ralph Waldo Emerson, *The Essential Writings of Ralph Waldo Emerson*, Brooks Atkinson, ed., p. 322.

[58] Langer, op. cit., p. 125.

[59] Geoffrey Scott, *The Architecture of Humanism*, p.159.

[60] Ibid., p. 162.

[61] Langer, op. cit., p. 125.

[62] Le Corbusier 1986, op. cit., p. 68. The original French reads: "La plupart des architectes n'ont-ils pas oublie aujourd'hui que *la grande architecture est origines memes de l'humanité* et qu'elle est fonction directe des instincts humains?" (Le Corbusier, *Vers Une Architecture*, Paris: Flammarion, 2006, p. 55.) A more literal translation of the italicized words is "great architecture *has the same origins* as humanity.

[63] Pawan Sinha, "Once Blind and Now They See", *Scientific American*, July 2013, pp. 49-55.

[64] Irvin Rock, *Perception, op.* cit., pp. 88-89.

[65] Rock, *The Logic of Perception* Cambridge, MA: The MIT Press,1985, p. 112.

[66] Ibid., p. 119.

[67] Pinker, op. cit., pp. 282-284. See also L.A.Cooper & R.N.Shepard, "Chronometric studies of the rotation on mental images," in *Visual Information Processing*, W.G.Chase (Ed.) New York: Academic Press, 1973.

[68] Roger N. Shepard and Jacqueline Metzler, "Mental Location of 3 Dimensional Objects" *Science*, Vol. 171, pp. 701-703. Licensed publisher, American Association of Science.

[69] Rudolf Arnheim, *Art and Visual Perception: the New Version*, 1974, op. cit., p. 263.

[70] Ibid., p. 261.

[71] Eric Kandel *The Age of Insight: The Quest To Understand The Unconscious In Art, Mind, and Brain, From Vienna 1900 To The Present.* New York: Random House, 2012, p. 283.

[72] J.V. Field, *The Invention of Infinity: Mathematics and Art in the Renaissance*", p. 26.

[73] Frank Wilczek, *A Beautiful Question*, pp. 137, 239, 279.

[74] Dehaene, Stanislav, *Reading in the Brain*, p. 269.

[75] The architect is not the only one to do this. Great painters like Cézanne and Vermeer do the same. Each of them frequently organize compositions that balance around the canvas' vertical centerline, and the centerlines are marked, sometimes subtly, sometimes not so.

[76] Birkhoff, George David. "A Mathematical Theory of Art", in *The World of Mathematics*, ed. by James R. Newman, pp. 76 2185-2198. New York:
Simon and Schuster, 1956.
Although Birkhoff appears to make his formulation rigorous enough to permit "measurable" results, such a goal would face formidable difficulties, and perhaps a fatal one, if the beholder's individual capacity for grasping "C" and "O" is taken into account. But the clarity of the simple formula, and the clarity with which it separates "associational" from "formal" values, give helpful discipline to the overarching .idea of "variety in unity."

[77] Frank Lloyd Wright, *Frank Lloyd Wright Collected Writings*, Vol. 2, "An Autobiography: Book Three", New York: Rizzoli, p. 372.

[78] Frank Wilczek, *A Beautiful Question*, op. cit., p. 14.

[79] Ibid., p. 15.

[80] Ibid., Figure 345.

[81] Robert McCarter, Frank Lloyd Wright (London and New York: Phaidon Press Limited, 1999), p.258.

[82] Pfeiffer 1993, op. cit., p. 222.

[83] Pfeiffer 1991, p. 132.

[84] Isaac Newton, *The Principia*, Amherst, New York: Prometheus Books, 1995, p. 19.

[85] By the law of Conservation of Energy, because the balls do not deform, total Kinetic Energy before and after the collision remains unchanged. Kinetic energy is a function of mass and velocity (½ the mass × the square of the velocity); because the two balls are identical in mass, the sum of the squares of the velocities of the two balls after the collision must equal the square of the velocity of the cue ball before. The velocities are vectors. The vector addition that will give us this equality is given by the Pythagorean theorem: the square of the original velocity of the cue ball will equal the sum of the squares of the velocities of the cue object ball and the object ball after the collision, if their resultant velocities are represented by the two sides of the right triangle formed with the original velocity as hypotenuse. The two balls must part at right angles!

[86] Max Born, *Einstein's Theory of Relativity*, Revised Ed. (New York: Dover Publications, Inc., 1965), p.164.

BIBLIOGRAPHY

Aguar, Charles E. and Berdeana. *Wrightscapes.* New York: McGraw- Hill, 2002.

Arnheim, Rudolf. *Art and Visual Perception.* Berkeley and Los Angeles: University of California Press, 1957.

Arnheim, Rudolf. "Gestalt Psychology and Artistic Form," in *Aspects of Form*, ed. by Lancelot Law Whyte. Bloomington: Indiana University Press, 1961.

Arnheim, Rudolf. *Visual Thinking.* Berkeley, Los Angeles, London: University of California Press, 1972.

Arnheim, Rudolf. *Art and Visual Perception: the New Version.* Berkeley and Los Angeles: University of California Press, 1974.

Arnheim, Rudolf. *The Dynamics of Architectural Form.* Berkeley, Los Angeles, London: University of California Press, 1977.

Belting, Hans. *Florence and Baghdad: Renaissance Art and Arab Science.* Cambridge, Massachusetts and London: The Belknap Press of Harvard University Press, 2011.

Biederman, Irving. "Visual Object Recognition", Chapter 4, pp. 121-166, in *Visual Cognition: and Invitation to Cognitive Science, Vol. 2*, op. c105it.

Birkhoff, George David. "A Mathematical Theory of Art", in *The World of Mathematics*, ed. by James R. Newman, pp. 2185-2198. New York: Simon and Schuster, 1956.

Born, Max. *Einstein's Theory of Relativity.* Revised Edition. New York: Dover Publications, Inc., 1965.

Bruce, Vicki, Patrick R. Green, Mark A. Georgeson. *Visual Perception.* 4th Ed. Hove and New York: Psychology Press, 2003.

Bultman, Scott. *The Froebel Gifts 2000.* Kindergarten Messenger, a division of American Traditional Toys, Inc., 2000.

Byrne, Oliver. *The First Six Books of the Elements of Euclid.* London: William Pickering, 1847. Facsimile edition: Los Angeles: Taschen, 2010.

Carter, Rita. *Mapping the Mind.* Revised and Updated Edition. Berkeley and Los Angeles: University of California Press, 2010.

Cleary, Richard; N. Levine, M. Marefat, B.B.Pfeiffer, J.M.Siry, and M. Stipe. *Frank Lloyd Wright: From Within Outward.* New York: Guggenheim Museum Publications, 2009.

Chatterjee, Anjan. *The Aesthetic Brain.* Oxford University Press, 2014.

Crease, Robert P. *The Great Equations.* New York: W.W. Norton & Company, Inc., 2008.

Danchev, Alex, Editor and Translator. *The Letters of Paul Cezanne.* Los Angeles: The J. Paul Getty Museum, 2013.

DeHaene, Stanislas. *The Number Sense.* Oxford and New York: Oxford University Press, 2009.

DeHaene, Stanislas. *Reading in the Brain.* New York: Viking, published by the Penguin Group, 2009.

Doran, Michael. *Conversations with Cézanne.* Berkeley, California: University of California Press, 2001

Devlin, Keith. *Mathematics: The Science of Patterns.* New York: Scientific American Library, distributed by W.H.Freeman and Company, 1994.

Einstein, Albert. *The Meaning of Relativity.* Princeton, New Jersey: The Princeton University Press, 1922-1953.

Einstein, Albert. *Ideas and Opinions.* New York: The Modern Library, 1954.

Emerson, Ralph Waldo, *The Essential Writings of Ralph Waldo Emerson.* Ed. by Brooks Atkinson. New York: The Modern Library, 2000. The epigraph for Chapter 1 occurs on page 268.

Elam, Kimberly. *Geometry of Design, 2nd Edition* New York: Princeton Architectural Press, 2011.

Fanelli, Giovanni. *Brunelleschi.* New York: Scala Books, distributed by Harper & Row, Publishers.

Feynman, Richard. *The Character of Physical Law.* Cambridge, MA: The M.I.T.Press, 1992.

Field, J.V. *The Invention of Infinity: Mathematics and Art in the Renaissance.* Oxford, New York, Tokyo: Oxford University Press, 1997.

Furnari, Michele. *Formal Design in Renaissance Architecture.* New York: Rizzoli International Publications, Inc., 1995.

Futagawa, Yukio, editor and photographer, and Bruce Brooks Pfeiffer, text. *Frank Lloyd Wright.* Monographs, vol. 1-12. Tokyo: A.D.A. Edita, c1984.

Gast, Klaus-Peter. *Louis I. Kahn: the Idea of Order.* Basil, Berlin, Boston: Brikhauser – Publishers for Architecture, 2001.
Gazzaniga, Michael S. *Tales From Both Sides of the Brain.* New York: Harper Collins Publishers, 2015.
Gifford, Don, ed. *The Literature of Architecture.* New York: E.P.Dutton & Co., Inc., 1966.
Gill, Robert W. *Perspective From Basic To Creative.* London: Thames & Hudson, 2006.
Goodale, Melvyn Alan. "The Cortical Organization of Visual Perception and Visuomotor Control", pp. 167-214, in *Visual Cognition: An Invitation to Cognitive Science, 2nd Ed.*, Volume 2, Op.Cit.
Gimpel, Jean. *The Cathedral Builders.* Trans. by Teresa Waugh. New York: Harper Perennial, 1992.
Greene, Brian. *The Fabric of the Cosmos: Space, Time, and the Texture of Reality.* New York: Vintage Books, 2005.
Guiton, Jacques. *The Ideas of Le Corbusier.* Trans. by Margaret Guiton. New York: George Braziller, 1981.
Hale, Jonathon. *The Old Way of Seeing.* New York: Houghton Mifflin Company, 1994.
Hitchcock, Henry-Russell. *In the Nature of Materials.* New York: Da Capo Press, 1975.
Hoffmann, Donald. *Frank Lloyd Wright's Robie House.* New York: Dover Publications, Inc., 1984.
Holt, Jim. "Annals of Science: Numbers Guy: Are Our Brains Wired for Math?" *The New Yorker* (March 3, 2008), pp.42-47.
Hubel, David H. *Eye, Brain, and Vision.* New York: Scientific American Library, 1988.
Kandel, Eric R. *The Age of Insight: The Quest To Understand The Unconscious In Art, Mind, and Brain, From Vienna 1900 To The Present.* New York: Random House, 2012.
Kandel, Eric R. *Reductionism in Art and Brain Science: Bridging the Two Cultures.* New York: Columbia University Press, 2016.
Kandel, Eric R., James H. Schwartz, Thomas M. Jessell, Steven A. Siegelbaum, A. J. Hudspeth, editors, *Principles of Neural Science, 5th Edition.* New York: The McGraw-Hill Companies, Inc., 2013.
Kosslyn, Stephen Michael and Daniel N. Osherson (ed.) *Visual Cognition: An Invitation to Cognitive Science, Second Edition, Vol. 2.* Cambridge, MA: The MIT Press, 1995.
Langer, Suzanne K. *Mind: An Essay on Human Feeling.* Baltimore: The Johns Hopkins Press, 1967.
Laseau, Paul and James Tice. *Frank Lloyd Wright: Between Principle and Form.* New York: Van Nostrand Reinhold, 1992.
Le Corbusier. *Towards a New Architecture.* Trans. and intro., Frederick Etchells. New York: Dover Publications, Inc., 1986. (1st publ. 1931).
Le Corbusier. *Vers Une Architecture.* Paris: Flammarion, 1995. (1st publ. in 1923).
Le Corbusier. *The Modular.* Trans. by Peter de Francia and Anna Bostick. Cambridge, Mass.: The MIT Press, 1968.
Le Corbusier. *Modular 2.* Trans. by Peter de Francia and Anna Bostick. Cambridge, Mass.: The M.I.T. Press, 1968.
Le Corbusier. *Le Modulor, Le Modulor 2.* (boxed set). In French. Basel, Boston, Berlin: Birkhäuser, 2000.
Lederman, Leon M. and Christopher T. Hill. *Symmetry and the Beautiful Universe.* Amherst, NY: Prometheus Books, 2004.
Levine, Neil. *The Architecture of Frank Lloyd Wright.* Princeton, New Jersey: Princeton University Press, 1996.
Livingstone, Margaret. *Vision and Art: The Biology of Seeing.* Revised and Expanded Edition. New York: Abrams, 2014.
Mallgrave, Harry Francis. *The Architect's Brain: Neuroscience, Creativity, and Architecture.* Malden, MA: Wiley-Blackwell; John Wiley & Sons, Ltd. Publications, 2011.
March, Lionel and Philip Steadman. *The Geometry of Environment.* London: RIBA Publications Limited, 1971.
Marr, David. *Vision.* New York: W. H. Freeman and Co., 1982.

Marr, David and H.K.Nishihara. *Representation and Recognition of the Spatial Organization of Three-Dimensional Shapes.* Proceedings of the Royal Society of London. Series B, Biological Sciences. Vol. 200, No.1140. (Feb. 23, 1978), pp.269-294.

McGilchrist, Iain. *The Master and his Emissary: the Divided Brain and the Making of the Western World.* New Haven and London: Yale University Press, 2009, pb 2010.

Meehan, Patrick J.A.I.A. ed. *Frank Lloyd Wright Remembered.* Washington, D.C.: The Preservation Trust, National Trust for Historic Preservation, 1991.

McCarter, Robert. *Fallingwater; Frank Lloyd Wright.* New York: Phaidon Press Limited, 1994.

McCarter, Robert. *Frank Lloyd Wright.* London and New York: Phaidon Press Limited, 1999.

McCarter, Robert (ed). *On and By Frank Lloyd Wright: A Primer of Architectural Principles.* London: Phaidon Press Limited, 2005.

McCarter, Robert and Juhani Pallasmaa. *Understanding Architecture: A Primer on Architecture as Experience.* London and New York: Phaidon Press Ltd. and Phaidon Press Inc., 2012.

Morton, Terry B., Editor. *The Pope-Leighey House.* Washington, D.C.: The Preservation Press, National Trust for Historic Preservation, 1983.

Newton, Sir Isaac. *The Principia.* Translated by Andrew Motte. Amherst, New York: Prometheus Books, 1995.

Orear, Jay. *Fundamental Physics.* 2nd Edition. New York: John Wiley & Sons, Inc., 1967.

Okakura, Kakuzo. *The Book of Tea.* Tokyo, New York, London: Kodansha International, 2005. (Written in 1906).

Osherson, Daniel N., Stephen M.Kosslyn, and John M.Hollerbach, (eds.). *Visual Cognition and Action, An Invitation to Cognitive Science, Vol. 2.* Cambridge, Massachusetts: The MIT Press, 1990.

Palmer, Stephen E. *Vision Science: Photons to Phenomenology.* Cambridge, Massachusetts and London: The MIT Press, 1999.

Pinker, Steven, (ed.) *Visual Cognition.* Cambridge, MA and London: The MIT Press, 1985 and 1986.

Pinker, Steven. *How the Mind Works.* New York and London: W.W.Norton & Company, 2009.

Pfeiffer, Bruce Brooks. *Frank Lloyd Wright.* Hong Kong, Köln, London, Los Angeles, Madrid, Paris, Tokyo: Taschen, 1991.

Pfeiffer, Bruce Brooks. *Frank Lloyd Wright: the Masterworks.* New York: Rizzoli International Publications, Inc., 1993.

Pfeiffer, Bruce Brooks, author; Peter Gössel, editor. *Frank Lloyd Wright: The Complete Works,* volumes 1, 2, and 3. Publisher, Taschen.

Ramachandran, V.S. and Sandra Blakeslee. *Phantoms in the Brain.* New York: Harper Perennial, HarperCollins Publishers Inc., 1998.

Ramachandran, V.S. *The Tell-tale Brain.* New York, London: W.W.Norton & Company, 2011.

Richardson, Robert D. *First We Read, Then We Write: Emerson on the Creative Process.* Iowa City: University of Iowa Press, 2009.

Rock, Irvin. *Perception.* New York: Scientific American Library, 1984.

Rock, Irvin. *The Logic of Perception.* Cambridge, MA: The MIT Press, 1985.

Rogers, Wallace J. *Frank Lloyd Wright's Samara.* Lafayette, IN: Lafayette Printing Company, 2001.

Sacks, Oliver.. *The Mind's Eye.* New York: Vintage Books, A Division of Random House, Inc., 2010.

Sacks, Oliver. *Hallucinations.* New York: Alfred A. Knopf, 2012.

Scott, Geoffrey. The Architecture of Humanism. Garden City, N.Y.: Doubleday & Company, Inc., 1924.

Scully Jr., Vincent. *Frank Lloyd Wright.* New York: George Braziller, Inc., 1960.

Scully Jr., Vincent. *Modern Architecture.* New York: George Braziller, Inc., 1961.

Sergeant, John. *Frank Lloyd Wright's Usonian Houses.* New York: Whitney Library of Design, an imprint of Watson-Guptill Publications, 1975.

Schrödinger, Ervin. *Collected Papers on Wave Mechanics.* New York: Chelsea Publishing Company, 1978.

Schrödinger, Ervin. "What is Matter?" *Scientific American.* Vol.189 (Sept. 1953), pp. 52-58.

Scientific American. *Mind.* Vol. 22, Number 3. New York: Scientific American, Fall 2013.

Scott, Geoffrey. *The Architecture of Humanism.* Garden City, N.Y.: Doubleday & Company, Inc., 1924.

Shepard, Roger N. and Jacqueline Metzler, "Mental Location of 3 Dimensional Objects", *Science,* vol. 171, pp. 701-703. Licenced publisher: American Association of Science.
Shimamura, Arthur P. and Stephen E. Palmer. *Aesthetic Science: Connecting Minds, Brains, and Experience.* Oxford University Press, 2014.
Sinha, Pawan. "Once Blind and Now They See", *Scientific American July 2013,* Volume 309, Number 1, pp.48-55.
Stein, Barry E., Editor. *The New Handbook of Multisensory Processing.* Cambridge, Massachusetts: The MIT Press, 2012.
Stoll, Robert. *Architecture and Sculpture in Early Britain.* Photographs by Jean Roubier. New York: The Viking Press, Inc., 1967.
Storrer, William Allin. *The Frank Lloyd Wright Companion.* Chicago and London: The University of Chicago Press, 1993.
Sullivan, Louis H. *A System of Architectural Ornament.* New York: Press of the American Institute of Architects, Inc., 1924. (Facsimile ed.: Park Forest, Il.: The Prairie School Press, 1964.) The epigraph for the book occurs on Plate 9.
Thompson, D'Arcy Wentworth. *On Growth and Form.* Cambridge: Cambridge University Press, 1963.
Yutang, Lin., translator and editor. *The Wisdom of Laotse.* New York: The Modern Library, 1948. The epigraph in Chapter 10 is found on page 214.
Weyl, Hermann. *Symmetry.* Princeton, New Jersey: Princeton University Press, 1952.
Whitehead, Alfred North. *Science and the Modern World.* New York: Macmillan Publishing Co., Inc., 1967.
Wilczek, Frank. *A Beautiful Question: Finding Nature's Deep Design.* New York: Penguin Press, 2015.
Wright, Frank Lloyd. *Architectural Forum.* Vol. 68 (January 1938), whole issue.
Wright, Frank Lloyd. *Architectural Forum.* Vol. 88 (January 1948), whole Issue.
Wright, Frank Lloyd. *The Future of Architecture.* New York: Horizon Press, 1953.
Wright, Frank Lloyd. *The Natural House.* New York: Horizon Press, Inc., 1954.
Wright, Frank Lloyd. *An American Architecture.* Edited by Edgar Kaufmann. San Francisco: Pomegranate, 2006. (1st published by Horizon Press, 1955).
Wright, Frank Lloyd. *A Testament.* New York: Bramhall House (1st published by Horizon Press, Inc., 1957.)
Wright, Frank Lloyd. *The Work of Frank Lloyd Wright.* 1965 Edition, New York: Horizon Press, 1965. (1st published by Wendingen, 1925)
Wright, Frank Lloyd. *Frank Lloyd Wright: Writings and Buildings.* Edited by Edgar Kaufmann and Ben Raeburn. New York: The World Publishing Co., 1972.
Wright, Frank Lloyd. *Frank Lloyd Wright: Collected Writings, Vol. 2.* Edited by Bruce Brooks Pfeiffer. NewYork: Rizzoli International Publications, Inc., 1992.
Wright, Frank Lloyd. "The Logic of the Plan", pp. 345-347 in McCarter, Robert, (ed.), *On and By Frank Lloyd Wright: a Primer of Architectural Principles".* London: Phaidon Press Limited, 2005.
Wright, Frank Lloyd. *The Essential Frank Lloyd Wright: Critical Writings on Architecture.* Edited by Bruce Brooks Pfeiffer. Princeton and Oxford: Princeton University Press, 2008.
Zeki, Semir. *A Vision of the Brain.* London: Blackwell Scientific Publications, 1993.
Zeki, Semir. *Inner Vision: An Exploration of Art and the Brain.* New York: Oxford University Press, 1999. The epigraph for Chapter 10 is found on p.10.
Zeki, Semir. *Splendors and Miseries of the Brain: Love, creativity, and the Quest for Human Happiness.* Oxford, UK: Wiley-Blackwell, a John Wiley & Son, Ltd., Publication, 2009.

ILLUSTRATION CREDITS

1.1 Pg. 75, *Towards a New Architecture* (Frederick A Praeger, New York, 1954) @ F.L.C./ADAGP, Paris / Artists Rights Society (ARS), New York 2018.

1.2 Pg.74, *Towards a New Architecture* @ F.L.C./ADAGP, Paris / Artists Rights Society (ARS), New York 2018.

1.3 Pg. 79, *Towards a New Architecture* @ F.L.C. / ADAGP, Paris / Artists Rights Society (ARS), New York 2018.

1.4 Pg. 252, *Frank Lloyd Wright: A Primer on Architectural Principles.* Courtesy of Robert McCarter.

1.5 Pg. 73, *Towards a New Architecture* @ F.L.C./ADAGP, Paris / Artists Rights Society (ARS), New York 2018.

1.6 Pg. 73, *Towards a New Architecture* @ F.L.C./ADAGP, Paris / Artists Rights Society (ARS), New York 2018.

1.7 Pg. 63, *Towards a New Architecture* @ F.L.C./ADAGP, Paris / Artists Rights Society (ARS), New York 2018.

1.8 Pg. 63, *Towards a New Architecture* @ F.L.C./ADAGP, Paris / Artists Rights Society (ARS), New York 2018.
Red overlay @John H. Shoaff 2018.

1.9 Pg. 224, *Modular 2* @ F.L.C./ADAGP, Paris / Artists Rights Society (ARS), New York 2018.

1.10 Pg. 218, *Modular 2* @ F.L.C./ADAGP, Paris / Artist Rights Society (ARS), New York 2018.

1.11 Pg. 56, *The Old Way of Seeing,* Courtesy of Jonathan Hale.

1.12 Pg. 358, *Frank Lloyd Wright: The Complete Works 1885-1916.* Copyright @ 2017 Frank Lloyd Wright Foundation, Scottsdale, AZ. All rights reserved. The Frank Lloyd Wright Foundation Archives (The Museum Modern Art|Avery Architectural & Fine Arts Library, Columbia University, New York).

2.1 Photograph supplied by author. The plan was copied from the original construction drawing from which the house was built. It varies from the plan shown as 5110.003 on pg. 240 of *Frank Lloyd Wright: The Complete Works 1943-1959,* Copyright @ Frank Lloyd Wright Foundation, Scottsdale, AZ. All rights reserved. The Frank Lloyd Wright Foundation Archives (The Museum Modern Art | Avery Architectural & Fine Arts Library, Columbia University, New York), which shows bedroom and pool-house additions that were never built.
Red-lined overlays: Copyright @John H. Shoaff 2018.

3.1 Perspective: 4116.001; plan 4116.009, pg. 357, *Frank Lloyd Wright: The complete Works 1917-1942.* Copyright@Frank Lloyd Wright Foundation Archives (The Museum of Modern Art | Avery Architectural & Fine Arts Library, Columbia University, New York.)
Red-lined overlays: Copyright @John H. Shoaff 2018.

3.2 Photograph: 0908.0024, page 360, *Frank Lloyd Wright: The Complete Works 1885-1916.* Photographer unknown. Plan is Plate 86 of the Warmuth Fascimile Copyright @ Frank Lloyd Wright Foundation, Scottsdale, AZ. All rights reserved. The Frank Lloyd Wright Foundation Archives (The Museum Modern Art | Avery Architectural & Fine Arts Library, Columbia University, New York).
Red-lined overlays: Copyright @John H. Shoaff 2018.

3.3 Photograph: Leavenworth's. Plan shown is as printed on pg. 102 of *The Natural House,* redrawn from 3907.007, pg. 389, *Frank Lloyd Wright: The Complete Works 1917-1942.* Copyright @ Frank Lloyd Wright Foundation Scottsdale, AZ. All rights reserved. The Frank Lloyd Wright Foundation Archives (The Museum Modern Art | Avery Architectural & Fine Arts Library, Columbia University, New York).
Red-lined overlays: Copyright @John H. Shoaff 2018.

4.1 By the author; all drawings in 4 after 4.2 and 4.3 are by the author.

4.2 Arnheim 1974, pg.13, @University of California Press. Courtesy of University of California Press.

4.3 Louis Sullivan 1924, Plate 1. Reproduced with permission of the American Institute of Architects. 1735 New York Avenue, NW, Washington, DC 20006.

5.1 Courtesy of Proceedings of the Royal Society of London, Series B, 200, 269-294 (1978). Permission conveyed through Copyright Clearance Center, Inc.=

5.2 Courtesy of Proceedings of the Royal Society of London, Series B, 200, 269-294 (1978). Permission conveyed through Copyright Clearance Center, Inc.

5.3 From Kosslyn, Stephen M. and Daniel N. Osherson, eds. *An Invitation to Cognitive Science, second edition, Volume 2,* p.140 @ 1995 Massachusetts Institute of Technology by permission of The MIT Press.

5.4 Courtesy of Proceedings of the Royal Society of London, Series B, 200, 269-294 (1978). Permission conveyed through Copyright Clearance Center, Inc.

5.5 Drawing by Robert W. Gill from Perspective: *from Basic to Creative,* pg. 137, Reproduced by kind permission of Thames & Hudson Ltd., London.

5.6 Drawing by Robert W. Gill from Perspective: *from Basic to Creative,* pg. 144. Reproduced by kind permission of Thames & Hudson Ltd., London.

5.7 *A Beautiful Question,* pg. 69. Copyright @ 2015 Frank Wilczek.

5.8 *The Logic of Perception,* pg. 112. Courtesy of Sylvia Rock.

5.9 *The Logic of Perception,* pg. 119. Courtesy of Sylvia Rock.

5.10 By permission of Shepard and Metzler, "Mental Location of 3 Dimensional Objects" in Science Vol. 171, pp. 701-703 (1971). Permission conveyed through Copyright Clearance Center, Inc.

5.11 Arnheim 1974, pg. 263, @University of California Press; by courtesy of University of California Press.

5.12 Arnheim 1974, pg. 261, @University of California Press; by courtesy of University of California Press.

5.13 *A Beautiful Question,* pg. 69. Copyright @ 2015 Frank Wilczek.

5.14 From *The Invention of Infinity,* pg. 26, @J.V. Field, 1997. Courtesy of J.V. Field.

6.1 Photograph by David Davison. Plan taken from *The Natural House,* pg.152; corresponds with 5012.006, pg. 278, *Frank Lloyd Wright: The Complete Works 1943-1959.* Copyright @ Frank Lloyd Wright Foundation Scottsdale, AZ. All rights reserved. The Frank Lloyd Wright Foundation Archives (The Museum Modern Art | Avery Architectural & Fine Arts Library, Columbia University, New York). Red-lined overlays: Copyright @John H. Shoaff 2018.

6.2 Perspective, pg. 80 and plan, pg. 81, from *Architectural Forum January 1938.* Except for its inclusion of the garden and bordering hedge, The plan is identical to 3702.022, pg. 280 of *Frank Lloyd Wright: The Complete Works 1917-1942.* Copyright @ Frank Lloyd Wright Foundation Scottsdale, AZ. All rights reserved. The Frank Lloyd Wright Foundation Archives (The Museum Modern Art | Avery Architectural & Fine Arts Library, Columbia University, New York.) Red-lined overlays:Copyright @John H. Shoaff 2018.

6.3 Photo, pg. 112, by G.E.Kidder-Smith; plan, pg. 110 in *The Natural House.* Plan corresponds with 3903.004, pg. 400, *Frank Lloyd Wright: The Complete Works 1917-1942.* Copyright @ Frank Lloyd Wright Foundation Scottsdale, AZ. All rights reserved. The Frank Lloyd Wright Foundation Archives (The Museum Modern Art | Avery Architectural & Fine Arts Library, Columbia University, New York.) Red-lined overlays:Copyright @John H. Shoaff 2018.

6.4 Photo from *An American Architecture,* pg. 47, uncredited. Plan taken from *Architectural Forum January 1948,* pg. 77. Copyright @ Frank Lloyd Wright Foundation Scottsdale, AZ. All rights reserved. The Frank Lloyd Wright Foundation Archives (The Museum Modern Art | Avery Architectural & Fine Arts Library, Columbia University, New York).
Red-lined overlays: Copyright @John H. Shoaff 2018.

6.5 Photograph: Beinert, plan: 4111.022, p. 420, *Frank Lloyd Wright: The Complete Works 1917-1942.* Copyright @ Frank Lloyd Wright Foundation Scottsdale, AZ. All rights reserved. The Frank Lloyd Wright Foundation Archives (The Museum Modern Art | Avery Architectural & Fine Arts Library, Columbia University, New York).
Red-lined overlays: Copyright @John H. Shoaff 2018.

6.6 Perspective: 4105.014, p. 460 and plan: 4105.013, p. 461, *Frank Lloyd Wright: The Complete Works 1917-1942.* Copyright @ Frank Lloyd Wright Foundation Scottsdale, AZ. All rights reserved. The Frank Lloyd Wright Foundation Archives (The Museum Modern Art | Avery Architectural & Fine Arts Library, Columbia University, New York).
Red-lined overlays: Copyright @John H. Shoaff 2018.

6.7 Photo, p. 185, by Jack Howe and plan, p. 184, are from The Natural House. The plan corresponds to 4814.007, p. 207 of *Frank Lloyd Wright: The Complete Works 1943-1959.* Copyright @ Frank Lloyd Wright Foundation Scottsdale, AZ. All rights reserved. The Frank Lloyd Wright Foundation Archives (The Museum Modern Art | Avery Architectural & Fine Arts Library, Columbia University, New York).
Red-lined overlays: Copyright @John H. Shoaff 2018.

6.8 Photograph: Roy E. Petersen. The plan is taken from pg. 245 of An American Architecture; it appears to be the same plan as 3807.003, pg. 320, *Frank Lloyd Wright: The Complete Works 1917-1942.* Copyright @ Frank Lloyd Wright Foundation Scottsdale, AZ. All rights reserved. The Frank Lloyd Wright Foundation Archives (The Museum Modern Art | Avery Architectural & Fine Arts Library, Columbia University, New York).
Red-lined overlays: Copyright @John H. Shoaff 2018.

6.9 Photograph: Ezra Stoller. Plan as shown on pg. 119 of *The Natural House.* Identical to 5314.021, pg. 341, *Frank Lloyd Wright: The Complete Works 1917-1942.* Both sources are Copyright @ Frank Lloyd Wright Foundation Scottsdale, AZ. All rights reserved. The Frank Lloyd Wright Foundation Archives (The Museum Modern Art | Avery Architectural & Fine Arts Library, Columbia University, New York).
Red-lined overlays: Copyright @John H. Shoaff 2018.

6.10 Photographer unknown. Plans as shown on pg. 208 of *The Natural House.* Ground floor plan corresponds to 5305.0002, pg. 296, *Frank Lloyd Wright: The Complete Works 1917-1942.* Both sources are Copyright @ Frank Lloyd Wright Foundation Scottsdale, AZ. All rights reserved. The Frank Lloyd Wright Foundation Archives (The Museum Modern Art | Avery Architectural & Fine Arts Library, Columbia University, New York).
Red-lined overlays: Copyright @John H. Shoaff 2018.

6.11 Photographer unknown. 3602.044 (1st floor plan), 3602.048 (2nd preliminary sketch), 3602.166 (1st preliminary sketch) 3602.157 (plans and elevation) are found on pp. 250-253, *Frank Lloyd Wright: The Complete Works 1917-1942.* Copyright @ Frank Lloyd Wright Foundation Scottsdale, AZ. All rights reserved.
Frank Lloyd Wright Foundation Archives (The Museum of Modern Art | Avery Architectural & Fine Arts Library, Columbia University, New York).
Red-lined overlays: Copyright @John H. Shoaff 2018.

7.1 Pg. 53, Jay Orear, *Fundamental Physics* 2nd Edition, 1967.

7.2 Ibed., pg. 53.

7.3 Pg. 177, Max Born, Einstein's Theory of Relativity, Courtesy of Dover Publications. Copyright @ 1962, 1965 by Dover Publications, Inc.

7.4 Pg. 185, Max Born, Einstein's Theory of Relativity, Courtesy of Dover Publications. Copyright @ 1962, 1965 by Dover Publications, Inc.

7.5 Pg. 156, *Architecture and Sculpture of Early Britain.* Photographer: Jean Roubier. Copyright @ 1967 Thames and Hudson, London.

7.6 Pg. 51, *Architecture and Sculpture of Early Britain.* Photographer: Jean Roubier. Copyright @ 1967 Thames and Hudson, London.

7.7 Pp. 42-43 Giovanni Fanelli, *Brunelleschi,* Copyright @ 1980 Scalo Istituto Fotografico Editoriale, Firenze.

CPSIA information can be obtained
at www.ICGtesting.com
Printed in the USA
LVHW071534271121
704622LV00006B/172

9 781950 659746